RACE,
RELIGION, &
MUSLIM IDENTITY
IN BRITAIN

RACE, RELIGION, & MUSLIM IDENTITY IN BRITAIN

by

DR MUHAMMAD ABDUL BARI

renaissance
P R E S S

PUBLISHED BY RENAISSANCE PRESS
Uplands Business Centre, Bernard Street, Swansea, SA2 0DR,
United Kingdom

Renaissance Press is the academic label of Awakening Publications

RENAISSANCE PRESS
Uplands Business Centre, Bernard Street, Swansea, SA2 0DR,
United Kingdom
P.O. Box 360009, Milpitas, CA 95036, United States of America

First Published in November 2004
Printed in the United Kingdom
Typeset in Bembo 11/14 [CP]

A catalogue record for this book is available from the British Library

RACE, RELIGION & MUSLIM IDENTITY
IN BRITAIN
Abdul Bari, Muhammad
p. cm.

Includes bibliographical references
ISBN 0 9543294 7 3

CP81.E7N92 2002
74.823410793- 02-54402 CIP

Tim, Nabeel, Pauline, Usama, and Shargil

Dr Muhammad Abdul Bari is an educationalist with a PhD and PGCE from King's College London and a Management degree from the Open University. He has worked as an Air Force Officer, Researcher in Physics, Science Teacher and now works as a SEN Specialist in London. He advises the Commission for Racial Equality (CRE), Office of the Deputy Prime Minister (ODPM), and London Mayor's Office on community/ faith issues. Dr Abdul Bari is a Former President of the Islamic Forum Europe (IFE) and currently the Deputy Secretary General of the Muslim Council of Britain (MCB) and Chairman of the East London Mosque. He writes extensively on youth and community issues and is author of *Building Muslim Families* and *The Greatest Gift: A Guide to Parenting*.

CONTENT

ACKNOWLEDGEMENTS

With the rapid transformation within the Muslim community over the last few decades many young people are now finding it difficult to navigate between the demands of their religion on one side and social pressure on the other. Thus, working with them and addressing the issues pertinent to their daily life are challenging, to say the least. This book is the outcome of my long-term involvement with the young Muslims of London through my voluntary and professional work. This has put me on a continuous learning curve in assessing my personal situation as well. The foremost amongst the issues facing a young Muslim is of course one of 'identity', which I have tried to address through the mirror of Islamic principles.

I am indebted to my wife, Sayeda, for her contribution and support in the process of writing this book. My deep appreciation goes to our four children, particularly the eldest daughter Rima, for their enthusiasm and occasional help in typing of the manuscript and enriched argument on the topic. Their first-hand experience in growing as young Muslims in Britain was invaluable to my understanding of the issue.

Prof Muhammad Anwar of Warwick University gave me invaluable advice on the first draft of the manuscript. I am grateful to the many people who had their share in helping me articulate my views. May Allah bless them and allow this book to help create a confident Muslim community at peace with the wider British society.

FOREWORD

It is a fact that Britain today is a multi-racial and multi-faith society. British Muslims (1.8m) are an integral part of this country.
Almost 60 percent of the Muslim population is now British born.
Most of them are British citizens and Muslims are the largest religious minority group in Britain. Muslims in Britain, however,
face certain issues as a minority. In particular, they have been
made the focus of attention by politicians, the media and others
after the tragic events of 11 September 2001 in the US. As a result
there is more hostility and discrimination against Muslims which
forces them to seek support from their own communities.

British Muslims are particularly concentrated in certain areas.
For example, 700,000 live in London, 150,000 in Birmingham
and 80,000 in Bradford. Within London's Tower Hamlets alone,
there is a 75,000 strong Muslim population. It is worth point-
ing out that British Muslims are not a homogeneous group. They
come from different countries, belong to different ethnic groups
and speak different languages. Also there are generational differences, and they have sometimes diverse views on various issues. It

is also important that British Muslims are seen in a global context. This means that what happens to Muslims in other countries has relevance to British Muslims in terms of the public perception of Muslims and the media coverage, which is generally negative and has a direct impact on those perceptions. As a result of the negative portrayal, the hostility and discrimination against Muslims has recently increased.

The 2001 Census and other recent surveys show that British Muslims, particularly of Bangladeshi and Pakistani origin, are one of the most deprived groups in Britain. For example, Muslim school leavers as well as their parents face very high unemployment rates compared with whites and others from the same areas. The unemployment rate for Muslim groups is almost three times as high as the rate for whites. This is partly due to racial and religious discrimination.

In education, although recently there has been some improvement, Muslim children are still facing disadvantages in terms of poor educational achievement and lack of facilities for the teaching of their religion and culture in schools. In this context, Muslim parents are also concerned that their children are not able to learn about their religion in state educational institutions except in a few Muslim state funded schools. Muslim independent schools and Muslim organisations provide such teaching facilities in mosques and community centres, but those activities are not enough.

British Muslims generally live in inner-city run down areas and are segregated from other communities. Housing segregation for Muslims has clear implications for the quality of schools and bad housing certainly affect health. The housing conditions of British Muslims are inferior compared to that of white people. In addition, the public services have, in the main, failed to meet the specific needs of Muslims in terms of Halal food, prayer facilities, religious holidays, single sex education and so on. There is also serious under-representation of Muslims in the national and local level decision-making process and in key agencies such as government, the health service, the judiciary and the media. For example, there are only two Muslims in the House of Commons, out of 659 MPs. However, to reflect the Muslim population in Britain, there should be at least 20 Muslim MPs.

Research evidence shows that there is now a shift from racial discrimination towards religious and cultural discrimination in Britain. However, despite the legislation in this country against racial discrimination for the last 39 years, ethnic minorities including Muslims are still victims of racial discrimination. Sometimes Muslims face multiple discrimination, racial, religious and gender.

The Race Relations Act 1976 and the Race Relations (Amendment) Act 2000 do not fully protect Muslims because religious discrimination is not unlawful in Britain. However, the new European Employment Directive which came into effect in December 2003 will protect Muslims and other groups from religious discrimination in employment, although not in other fields. Religious discrimination is also taking place in the provision of services and other areas. Therefore, it is important that there is a comprehensive primary legislation against religious discrimination to protect Muslims and other religious communities in Britain.

There is a visible change in terms of the numbers from the first generation migrants to the second and third generation British born Muslims. This has resulted in an ongoing discussion within the Muslim communities in Britain about the question of identity and loyalty. Dr Abdul Bari has discussed this issue in detail in Chapter 9 'Muslim identity in Britain'. In this context it is worth mentioning that the Queen commenting on Muslim identity while on a state visit to Pakistan, said in a speech in Islamabad on 8 October 1997, 'A distinctive new identity that of the British Muslim, has emerged. I find that healthy and welcome'. However, we know from research that Muslims are generally misunderstood by non-Muslims in Britain, their loyalty to this country is often questioned and they face problems in terms of integration. Their difference of opinion on some current policies and issues is interpreted as disloyalty to this country. This is certainly not true and British Muslims are loyal citizens. However, young Muslims generally feel that they are being treated as second-class citizens. They also feel that their parents have, on the whole, tolerated prejudice, discrimination and harassment. It appears that young Muslims are not prepared to accept such racial and religious discrimination and harassment.

Unless young Muslims receive equal treatment, the tensions between them and non-Muslims are likely to grow as was seen in street disturbances in Oldham, Burnley and Bradford in the summer of 2001. A report after the disturbances showed that communities in those areas had become segregated in housing, education and employment, with differences in the way they spend leisure time, and that this had contributed to the breakdown of trust and cohesion. Therefore, positive policies and actions are needed by the state agencies and others to help the process of integration of British Muslims by establishing their rights and working and living conditions in line with those of their fellow-citizens. In addition, there needs to be more dialogue between Muslims and non-Muslims and in particular, engaging with young Muslims in various ways is critical in order to create community cohesion in the future.

I commend this book because Dr Abdul Bari has discussed

important issues concerning race and religion and how they relate to British Muslims historically and in the current political climate. The book makes a significant contribution to our knowledge about race relations in Britain as well as about British Muslims.

Professor Muhammad Anwar
Centre for Research in Ethnic Relations
University of Warwick
July 2004

INTRODUCTION

The twin issues of race and religion are central to western political and social agendas. This is in part due to the Renaissance and ensuing Enlightenment in Europe which marginalised the role of religion in state affairs, making race and racism the determining factors during Europe's dealings with weaker nations in the colonial period. The result was subjugation of lands, enslavement of human beings and violation of human dignity for hundreds of years. The two world wars of the 20th century, which originated in Europe due to extreme nationalism, were, in essence, rooted in their perception of racial superiority over others. European countries lost their colonies in the middle of the twentieth century due to the destruction they themselves inflicted on one another. Post-colonial Europe and other western nations then came to terms with the massive migration of Asian and African people to their countries. These immigrants were needed to sustain Europe's devastated economies, once again, bringing the issue of race to Europe's doorstep, albeit in a different manner. Things have changed significantly from the formation period of immigrant communities in western countries; hence the debate has taken a new turn.

In Britain issues related to race and racism have dominated the political scene since the 1950s. Successive Conservative and Labour governments[1] have felt it necessary to enact various Immigration Acts and Race Relations Acts to deal with immigration and ensuing race problems in society. These Acts thus became milestones in the attempt to tackle racial discrimination and racism in public life. With the formation of the Commission for Racial Equality (CRE) the race industry endeavoured to set the scene for a multicultural pluralist society in Britain on the basis of race and ethnicity. However, how far they have succeeded in eradicating racial discrimination and racism in Britain is debatable.

During this time another debate gained momentum behind the scenes in Britain and some other western countries. With the arrival of the first immigrants from Commonwealth countries, religious centres such as mosques, temples and Gurudwaras began to take root in the British landscape. Wherever Muslims, Hindus, Sikhs and people of other religious groups of 'Eastern' origin settled, they displayed their religious and cultural manifestations with resilience. Although these first generation Asians and Africans were identified as racial groups by the political establishment they refused to compromise their religious and cultural components of their identity for just one aspect of their identity, i.e. racial. While they were not unhappy, as such, in being labelled as racial or ethnic groups, they were keen to identify themselves as religious groups. Their refusal to be identified purely on the basis of race or geographic origin became a source of inspiration for others. Europe's Judeo-Christian heritage that had been marginalised under the hammer of secularism and atheism for many centuries, found new allies in the immigrant non-white people who upheld their religion and faith with openness and unbending seriousness. This emboldened the hitherto docile religious establishments in Britain, and together they forged an understanding and, in cases, alliances to put faith and religion back at the forefront of the social and political agenda.

Consequently, alongside the numerous existing Christian and Jewish establishments there emerged many organisations related with other religions. With these came the need for faith schools, the demand for religiously approved dress for school children of some communities, the necessity for dietary varieties, the need for recognition of religious celebrations and other ostentatious features.

The establishment of national organisations like the Interfaith Network in 1987 and the Inner Cities Religious Council in 1992 furthered the faith agenda.[2] The combined efforts of these groups achieved tangible successes in the recognition of faith and religion in public life. The inclusion of a religion question in the 2001 Census, though put as a voluntary question, was one of them. Although the Race Relations Act (RRA) 1976 and Race Relations (Amendment) Act (RRAA) 2000 are not explicit in recognising the cultural and religious identity of people, the changing nature of social dynamics has catapulted religion to take a prominent place in the public domain. The influence of religion in the curriculum remains erratic, but the inclusion of a citizenship curriculum in British schools from September 2002 has emphasised the importance of culture and religion in the country. The Parekh Report,[3] The Future of Multi-Ethnic Britain commissioned by the Runnymede Trust in 2000, has similarly highlighted the diversity of race, religion and culture of Britain.

Events around the world have also contributed to the religious debate in Britain. In the World Conference Against Racism

(WCAR) in Durban in September 2001 delegates maintained[4] that the increased salience of religion in race relations was now a world-wide phenomenon. In a sinister way, individual and group acts of terrorism in the name of religion, and the disproportionate retaliation from the state, have also highlighted that religion impacts not only on individual and communal life but also on global peace and security. Distressingly, the bigots on either side seem to have the upper hand at this period.

For the British Muslim community, the last 15 years were particularly testing. Some national and international events brought vulnerability and new challenges for them. The Rushdie affair of 1989, the first Gulf War of 1991, the genocide of Balkan Muslims in Bosnia Herzegovina and Kosovo in the mid-1990s, the formation of a Muslim umbrella group, the Muslim Council of Britain (MCB) in 1997 and the Runnymede Trust's report on Islamophobia in the same year put Muslims in the limelight. Then came the disturbances in the summer of 2001 in some cities of northern England in which some Muslim youth of South Asian origin clashed with police. The terrorist attack on America on September 11 in the same year created an unprecedented challenge for Muslims.

Massive events like these and subsequent repercussions have pushed Muslims to the sharp end of the debate. Events such as the heavy-handed and media-focused police raid on London's Finsbury Park Mosque in January 2003, the highly publicised security operation that brought army tanks to Heathrow airport, the insensitive press release by the Metropolitan Police on the day of the Muslim festival of *Eid-ul-Adha* two weeks later, the high profile arrests (complete with sensational headlines) of British Muslims allegedly linked with bio-terrorism – and other insensitive steps have created a siege mentality among many

Muslims. The negative portrayal of Muslims is being used as the rallying cry by the fascists and fanatics to 'fish in the muddy water' and to divide society. In the absence of a law to protect Muslims from incitement to religious hatred the Muslim community is experiencing a period of religious intolerance in Britain. The Madrid bombing on 11th March 2004, allegedly perpetrated by North African Arabs, killed nearly two hundred people fuelled the fire of suspicion against the Muslim community in Britain.

Muslim leaders in Britain have been demanding greater responsibility from politicians and the media in using terminology that could tarnish the image of Islam and victimise the Muslim community. In the wake of the Madrid bombing - and subsequent arrests in Britain - some senior politicians and a section of the media went out of their way in using terminology, such as 'Islamic terrorists', that questioned the community.

The police forces were also urged by Muslim community leaders to show more respect and sensitivity while arresting people, as too many terror suspects happen to be Muslims - despite only a few of them being charged under the terrorism act and a negligible number being convicted. Britain's largest Muslim umbrella group, The Muslim Council of Britain, questioned the home secretary whether these raids were mere 'fishing expeditions' and requested him to assure the Muslim community that it was not the case, which he did. But, in spite of repeated assurances from people in power, Muslims are still getting a raw deal. Young Muslims, particularly from Arab and South Asian communities are now facing increasing number of 'stop and search' operations by the police.[5] Ominously, for the first time, over forty Muslim graves were desecrated in South East London on 18th March 2004.

Adding insult to all these injuries, Muslims unexpectedly received some 'advice' from two senior clergymen, the former archbishop Lord Carey at a conference in Rome on 25th March 2004 and the Catholic bishop Cardinal Cormac Murphy O'Connor supporting Lord Carey's views two weeks later. Muslim leaders were bemused with this patronising 'advice', similar in tone with some neo-Cons in America, that Muslims would be better off if they embarked on a reformation of their religion in the way Christianity was reformed a few hundred years ago. Muslims consider this outrageous, not because they do not want modernisation of Muslim societies and contextual application of their religion, but because Muslims are not in the habit of changing their religion. Islam is a rational and pragmatic religion and has the ability to accommodate with time and space without changing its fundamentals. Muslims believe that while humans have shortcomings, Islam, the way of submission to God is perfect. However, this is altogether a different topic.

The *hijab* ban in French schools has been a major factor that has raised anxiety among British Muslims and, although senior figures in the British government have assured that Muslims in Britain have nothing to fear on this, they are concerned about the rising trend of Islamophobia in some parts of Europe as well as the level of ignorance and misunderstanding about Islam in general.

The atrocities against Muslims in some parts of the world and the British government's foreign policies towards the Muslim world are other factors that have caused anguish among many Muslim youth. The British support for the illegal US-led invasion of Iraq, the one time centre of Muslim civilisation, and now the brutality of occupation, the British green signal to the Israeli plan of legitimising its occupation of Palestinian lands are important sources of anguish and frustration of the Muslim community in Britain.

The immigration and asylum policy of the present Labour government has also caused disquiet among Muslims. Muslims constitute the largest proportion of refugees in the world, either due to the tyrannical regimes supported by the West or due to wars imposed on them. Any negative debate, especially on asylum, is bound to bring a negative image of Muslims. Unfortunately, due to the injustices done on many nations, asylum seeking in developed western countries would continue and Britain being an attractive destination cannot ignore the question for some time.

A combination of the above mentioned has created a challenge for the establishment, as well as the Muslim leadership in Britain. A recent Guardian/ICM poll published a worrying, but not unexpected, message of increasing sense of isolation among the Muslim community. Many in the Muslim community, not least from the second and third generation young Muslims, feel that the 'war on terrorism' is in fact a 'war against Islam'.[6]

Muslims, however, have so far been resilient in the defence of their community and their religion. Apart from a tiny minority of hotheads the whole community displayed a unique sobriety and firmness. They have rather been ahead in their expression of unilateral social responsibility in denouncing terrorism and defending peace and harmony in the wider British society. The Muslim Council of Britain's historic letter[7] on 31st March 2004 to the Imams and leaders of the mosques with a reminder to be vigilant on terrorism and to play their positive role in the society was one step ahead of other communities. It was a reminder to the Islamophobes that no amount of distraction would undermine the continuous Muslim commitment of human values, e.g., law and order, family and community ethos, enterprise and positive social harmony. Muslims would speak out whenever and wherever there is injustice and oppression, but in a lawful and civilised manner. They would do this as part of their religious obligation.

In this charged state of affairs, the issue that has been kicking for some time within the Muslim community, especially among the youth, is that of identity. In fact, this issue came to prominence in Britain three decades ago with the 'rivers of blood' speech by the Conservative politician Enoch Powell, and, later, by comments from others, including remarks by another Conservative politician, Norman Tebbit, in the 1980s. These comments made headlines in the media and contributed to the sense of disappointment within minority communities. However, in the 1970s and 1980s the debate was focussed primarily on the 'Asian' communities. What makes the present debate on identity so crucial is its global nature and that it seems to be primarily concerned with Muslims. This has become a 'religious' issue.

Where does the Muslim loyalty lie in Britain? Are they 'Muslim', 'British', 'Asian' or African? Which comes first?

It is now evident that a section of the media and some self-styled 'experts of Islam' in western countries have found a new 'bad guy' after the demise of Communism. It is the Muslim community that is expected to explain everything. The tragic events of September 11 have given this pretext and ammunition to do this. Muslims and other civil rights campaigners may find this selective debate patronising, but it is a challenge for not only the Muslim community but for all, as its ramifications are wide. It is sad that Muslims are singled out to answer certain questions others are not asked. It is also sad that fringe elements of the Muslim community are given disproportionate media coverage only to demonise Muslims.

Why is this question of identity hurled only at Muslims; as to whether they are Muslim first or British first? Is this question of loyalty, i.e., 'faith before country' or 'country before faith', necessary. Does it arise for other people, say, for Christians or Jews? Are the patriotic credentials of other communities questioned in the way they are with Muslims? These are a few of the counter questions many Muslims ask.

In any case, Muslims need to address these issues with the aid of robust Islamic principles and historical perspective. It is a soul-searching debate for the Muslim community and is has nothing to lose in this. If addressed holistically and with proper context it will not only benefit Muslims but also other people. The debate might have started from a negative premise of singling out one particular community, but Muslims have to accept that this is the nature of the game at this period of history. The Muslim community thus needs to be respectful and intelligent in engaging in this debate.

Faith and nationality that define the macro-identity of an individual or a community are fundamentally important. Each one has its demands, but at the end of the day it is the sense of humanity and justice that should prevail. Many white Christians in apartheid South Africa raised their voice against their state's policies and, similarly, some Jews in Israel, and people of other religions in many countries, go against their own government's policy because their religious principles lead them to espouse fair dealing and justice. Not long ago, many prominent American Christians refused to support their government's illegal war on Vietnam. That did not make them un-American. Faith guides one's conscience, actions and perspectives on life. People with or without faith use their conscience in defining moments to uphold peace, justice and humanity. There does not arise a necessity to make a choice between faith and no faith and between national or religious identities in those situations.

Identity is essential for human beings. It gives them anchor, root and a sense of belonging. Identity is linked with one's background and history. It helps people in their present and leads them to the future. The primary identity, according to Islam, is one's relationship with God and His creation.[8] In the conscious or subconscious mind religion plays a very deep and broad role. For Muslims religion encompasses all aspects of life - from personal hygiene to international dealings. However, contrary to racial or ethnic identity, faith and religious identity are a matter of choice, free from one's uncontrollable facets of life, such as one's ethnic or geographic root. Human beings have no control over their racial, ethnic or geographic identity. But faith or religious identity is dictated by one's deliberate acceptance of a pattern or way of life. This aspect of identity is not necessarily in conflict with other aspects. Different aspects of identity have different allegiances. What one needs to do is conscientiously navigate in different life situations. They are not mutually dependent on each other. As such, there is no dichotomy in one's Muslim identity with his or her other forms of identity. Muslims have been living as majority as well as minority communities in many parts of the world throughout history, albeit without compromising their religious principles and also without clashing with other aspects on their identity. Why should it be difficult now in the present day West?

With many communities in their midst, western countries now pride themselves on being multi-cultural, multi-faith and pluralistic. In Britain, there have been some positive changes in race relations over the past few decades. Religious pluralism is also becoming more and more prominent. After the adoption of the Race Relations Acts, incorporation of the Human Rights Act, and the inclusion of religion in the 2001 census, multiculturalism is achieving some moral strength in society. With the implementation of Article 13 of the European Employment Directives in December 2003, religious discrimination in employment was outlawed in Britain. However, more needs to be done on the policy fronts to create confidence in bringing about effective social inclusion of faith communities. At the same time, communities also need to come forward to dispel fear of one another. The older and more structured communities, e.g. Christians and Jews, have more responsibilities in this regard. The newer communities, e.g., Muslims and Hindus, need capacity building and empowerment within them so that their participation in social inclusion becomes meaningful. In order to create a 'rainbow' or 'mosaic' culture in the British social landscape, minority communities need to have the confidence that they will not suffer from overt or covert prejudice and discrimination from the establishment or dominant community. Young people from minority communities should be allowed to feel comfortable with their religious and ethnic identity.

It is understood that due to the structural weaknesses of the secular capitalist system the challenge against multiculturalism and social inclusion will not die away. The disturbances of summer 2001 which caused new challenges to positive community relationships are cited by some in authority, as the failure of multiculturalism. The proponents of a 'melting pot' culture or *assimilationist* agenda would always blame one or another section of the society to achieve their goal.

Like other youth in a society, Muslim youth have their difficulties. Some of them find difficulty coping in changing and complex social dynamics. However, there is no single reason for any social issue. It is now widely accepted that the main reason behind delinquency or even violent behaviour of some Muslim youth is unemployment, bad housing, deprivation, disaffection, discrimination, racism and similar factors. The 2001 Census has shown that Britain's Muslim community has a higher proportion of youth population and even second and third generation Muslims face multiple difficulties. With drugs, gang culture, and other negative influences around, some of them gradually lose their links with the roots of Islamic values and culture. The amoral dominant culture of the post-modern society on the one hand and continuous demonisation of their religion and culture by a section of the media on the other, prove too much for them. Those who have a strong anchor in the family and community with faith in their hearts have enough self-esteem and confidence to stay away from social diseases. Those who do not have that opportunity, young people from the Muslim and other vulnerable communities, express their alienation in a negative manner; they act in anti-social ways.

Islam encourages interaction, engagement and full participation with all people in society. By its very nature the religion of Islam is outgoing and, as such, it wants Muslims to create links with other human beings so that a collective sense of responsibility determines their positive behaviour towards the earth and its environment. With religious identity as the primary source of confidence and pride, Muslims are encouraged to make meaningful contribution to the society in which they live, and to work for justice and common values. Confident Muslims are not worried about their Islam or their survival as a community. Their job is not confined to defend themselves or their culture alone, but to co-exist with others to proactively defend all from immorality and injustice. They work for a common positive destiny of peace and justice for human beings on earth.

Islam requires Muslims to be at the heart of communal life. Their neighbourhood and social life as well as their economic and political activities are not bound by the interests of their own community alone, but for the wider society. Any policy of *ghettoisation* is borne out of ignorance and lack of confidence. It has become a disease of some recent Muslims, not only in the West but also in other parts of the world. The situation is gradually improving.

However, this does not mean that Muslims should not be careful about their distinctness of principle and unwittingly opt for total assimilation or dissolution in the dominant culture of any society. This is also foreign to them. Ghettoisation and assimilation are both anathema to them. In fact, most ghettoisation leads to assimilation unless a community physically moves to a different place. With such a rich Islamic heritage this cannot be an option for the Muslims of Britain.

The Muslim community is diverse and it comprises of various communities within itself.[9] The best way to protect Muslim identity is for Muslims to build a dynamic and vibrant community of their own in the first place and at the same time engage with others to create a safer and respectful civil society for all human beings. The necessity to build a just and peaceful society based on mutual rights and responsibilities is felt by all. This is a noble task that needs to be shared by all communities. Muslims can contribute to this only if they are equipped with confidence in their positive identity as Muslims.

This book addresses some of the basic issues surrounding Muslim identity in the context of race and religion. It deals with the issue of race, race relations and the challenges of pluralism in contemporary Britain. It addresses the question of religion, religious pluralism and the influence of faith and religion in British public life with an emphasis on the emerging nature of the Muslim community. It also discusses the contentious topic of identity in public life with various aspects of Muslim identity and social responsibility from an insider's point of view. The book aims to create understanding between communities and, as such, is useful for

Muslim and non-Muslim readers.

Before comencing, here are two brief notes. First, it is required by Muslim readers to recite a supplication (translated as 'God bless him and grant him peace') when they come across the names of Prophet Muhammad or any other Prophet. Second, the words 'race' and 'ethnicity' are not exactly the same and have different meanings. This also is the case with the terms 'faith' and 'religion'. However, they have often been used interchangeably in the book for the sake of simplicity.

I. RACE & RACISM IN HISTORY

Race and Ethnicity

'Race' is defined as a biological grouping within the human species possessing genetically transmitted traits that are sufficient to characterise it as a distinct human type'.[10] The modern understanding of race has originated from the global expansion of post-Renaissance European power in the form of colonialism and economic dominance. Politicians, social leaders, biologists and historians have used the term for various purposes. Race is considered by some as a genetic characteristic, such as hair colour, eye colour, etc. Some races constitute language groups, consisting of people with a common language, e.g., the Aryan race. The Semitic race was defined primarily to describe people who spoke Semitic languages. Some religious groups are also called races, e.g., the Jews and the Sikhs. Race has also been linked with various national or cultural groupings. In the census and other applications, 'race' often groups people for administrative convenience, e.g., Indian, African, White European, who may differ considerably in their racial origins. The concept and usage of the word varies with culture and geographical location of people. Needless to say, human beings constitute one human race.

The misuse of the word 'race', particularly during Nazi rule in Germany, has led people to look for alternative terms. The most common term often used with similar biological meaning is 'ethnic group', which generally means cultural or political groupings. With the advent of population genetics, some prefer the word 'population'.

With human genes constantly flowing from one gene pool to another, the human race is in a continuous state of change. With migration and marriage, races are being transformed continually since the beginning of human civilisation. This process of 'admixture' is influenced and dictated by political and economic factors, population pressure, war and other factors now related to globalisation. Human beings have now come to such a stage that there are no 'pure' races. Racial groups are now thoroughly mixed. There are small or large groupings of human beings. Geographic races are numerically large, containing within them smaller groups.

Due to ignorance and arrogance people of one race often find reasons to belittle others on the basis of their physical features, behaviour, language, and other cultural attributes. This stigmatisation of racial groups is the source of prejudice in the world, past and present. Racist jokes have always featured in popular culture in many countries. Often, people of one group regard people of another group unfavourably and sometimes even consider them inferior in intelligence. Victors of war generally treat the defeated with indignation, as being of lower intellect and less capable. At one time, there were even intellectual arguments as to whether the slaves in the European colonies had souls.

Such views gave rise to 'ethnocentrism', i.e., the idea that one's culture is superior to that of others', in the West. Darwin's theory of evolution and natural selection that promoted the 'survival of the fittest' principle became the hallmark of 'Social Darwinism' in human species. This gave intellectual comfort to many powerful and racist people in their repugnant and immoral exploitation of the weaker people in history. Racism thus still remains strong in many developed countries.

The ethnocentric European mindset remained convinced of the higher intellectual capacities of the Europeans. Intelligence tests, first used in the beginning of the twentieth century seemed to confirm that the English were more intelligent than others. It was later recognised that language, culture and socio-economic factors influenced the results of these tests. Modern genetics has revealed the folly of ethnocentrism and transformed our understanding of race in human species. It has also discarded the so-called 'evidence' that racial differences have direct effects on behaviour and culture. It is now agreed that communities subjected to humiliation over generations display a lot of weaknesses, not related with their racial background. As such, there is no justification for the superiority or inferiority between human beings on the basis of race. This view of race has resonance in the following verse from the Qur'an: 'O humankind! We created you from a male and female, and made you into peoples and tribes so that you might come to know each other. The noblest among you in Allah's sight is the one with the most God-consciousness.'[11]

Human beings are diverse and each one of them has unique features unlike anybody else. From the biological point of view, they were divided into major groups of races in accordance with their physical features, e.g., colour of skin, nasal shape, hair type, lip form, etc. This view was given prominence in nineteenth century scientific studies, according to which most human beings were classified roughly into nine large groupings of geographic races,[12] e.g., Caucasoid, Mongoloid, Negroid, Indic, Australoid, Polynesian, Micronesian, Melanesian, etc. Within these large groupings again, there are differences. With mixed marriages and migration, human beings have become more diverse than they were several hundred years ago.

'Ethnicity' is a modern concept which can be traced back to the colonial and post-colonial European dominance in the world. The word 'ethnic' comes from the Greek word *ethnos* meaning tribe. The term was derived from the fact that human beings cannot simply be grouped in terms of their genetic composition, they need to be commonly identified as social groups according to their distinctive cultural features, such as language, culture and institutions. Accordingly, for a group of people to qualify as an ethnic group they should have a long, shared history and cultural tradition of their own. Social groups can claim their ethnic uniqueness or may have it imposed upon them by dominant groups in a society. Ethnic groups thus reflect the political reality of a country, e.g. Sikhs and Jews in Britain.

Ethnicity is the community alliance through which members of a national, racial or religious grouping maintain an identity with people of the same community in a variety of official and unofficial ways. This also differentiates them from the other. There are 'three main ways in which ethnicity can survive. They are residence patterns whereby members of the same groups reside together; marriage patterns in which immigrants and their children marry within their own grouping; and religious and social activity'.[13]

The difference between race and ethnicity is often pedantic. The terms are often taken synonymously in the political and social context. Most nation states today consist of people from diverse ethnic backgrounds where there would be some minority communities. As human beings are inter-dependent, a successful society acknowledges the worth of all the communities and creates a legal basis for their equal treatment. The terms used for minority people in Britain are 'Minority Ethnic' communities or 'Black and Minority Ethnic' (BME) communities. 'A minority is a group of people distinguished by physical or cultural characteristics, subject to different and unequal treatment by the society in which they live and who regard themselves as victims of collective discrimination'.[14]

'Tribe' consists of people based on small groups defined by traditions of common descent and having temporary or permanent political feature and a shared language, culture, and ideology. Tribes are usually composed of a number of smaller local communities, e.g., villages, or neighbourhoods, and may form nations. Tribes may derive their unity from a sense of extended kinship, rather than from a territorial identity. The terms 'tribe' and 'ethnic group' may also be synonymous, depending on the situation. The latter is particularly appropriate in the modern context.

'Clans' are kinship groups the membership of which is socially defined in terms of descent from a common ancestor. The lineage could be traced through the father or mother. People clinging to their clan are strong in their view of the purity of lineage. Clan membership may be useful in ensuring mutual support and defence as well as in the mediation of internal disputes. Previous societies were known for their loyalty to tribes and clans. But in post-industrial European countries that has loosened a lot. This has been further sidelined in the modern technological countries of the West. The Eastern agrarian societies are variously maintaining their tradition regarding tribe and clan, but with rapid modernisation and urbanisation under the influence of globalisation this is now facing dilution.

The caste system, still prominent in countries like India, is the social stratification in which people are hierarchically separated from each other due to their descent, marriage and occupation.[15] The Porto-Spanish word *'Casta'* and the Indian word *'Jati'* mean 'race', 'breed' or 'lineage'. In some societies ethnic groups are also termed as castes. Each caste has its own customs that restrict the occupations and dietary habits of its members from social contacts with members of other castes. The lowest strata are the 'untouchables' *('Harijan'* in India) who are generally excluded from power, prestige and wealth of the society. The Hindu caste system is ancient and consists of four major castes, the *Brahmin* (priests and scholars), *Kshatriya* (warriors and rulers), *Vaisya* (merchants, traders, and farmers) and *Sudra* (the untouchables), where the major castes are subdivided into smaller sub-castes.

Hundreds of years of Muslim rule and almost two centuries of British colonial administration have had some impact on the caste system in India, and the strict separation of different castes has now loosened. On the other hand, India's Muslims, Sikhs, and Christians have also been influenced by the system and inadvertently adopted some of it in their cultures. Today however, the Indian constitution outlaws the 'untouchable' category and guarantees legal equality for all citizens.

Racial Pride in the Past

The issue of race and racial pride is as old as human civilisation. Those who were able to build empires with their hard work and their material supremacy often thought that they were of a superior race. The conquered people were often enslaved and treated with harshness and ignominy. The known ancient empires – the

Greek, Persian, Chinese, Indian, Roman and others – had substantial arrogance in their time on the basis of their perceived racial supremacy which they believed gave them the licence to subjugate other human beings.

In ancient Egypt, Babylon and other centres of civilisations the ruling classes used to claim divinity so that they could establish their monopoly and legitimacy of rule over the common people. This racial pride was based solely on one's birth, not on merit. There were 'master races' to rule and the slaves, including the commoners, to follow. The Persians were known to be great believers in the purity of their blood and superiority of their race. In India the upper-caste *Brahmins* were elevated to divinity and the untouchable *Sudras* were treated in the worst possible manner. The Arab society was torn apart by tribalism and tribal conflict, based on genealogical difference. Tribal loyalty or *'Asabiya'* was at the centre of their social system and they used to live and die for it. Racial prejudice was so strong in their psyche and their horizon of life was so painfully limited that they remained in the periphery of great empires and civilisations in history. Similarly, in the Roman Empire non-Romans were treated with contempt.

Prominent religious figures on the one hand and many philosophers and saints on the other, struggled to bring racial equality among human beings. Their efforts and sacrifices contributed to social and intellectual movements at different periods of history. Like other Prophets in the past, Prophet Muhammad also undertook this monumental task of eradicating racial arrogance from society. When Arabia was ripe with this scar, he declared in his farewell sermon that 'there is no superiority for an Arab over a non-Arab or for a non-Arab over an Arab, nor for the white over the black nor for the black over the white, except on the basis of God-consciousness'. That set the tone of equality between human beings for many centuries to come.

The message of those great individuals was simple – 'although human beings originate from the same source, they are diverse and there is no superiority of one over another'. The Renaissance ushered a new hope of human equality in Europe which culminated in the message of 'liberty, equality and fraternity' of the French Revolution. However, this universal message was not universal in post-Renaissance Europe. It mostly remained limited to white Europeans alone and failed to include non-White people. The mentality of many Europeans in the colonial era was reflected in Rudyard Kipling's poem, 'The White Man's Burden'.[16]

> Take up the White Man's Burden –
> Send forth the best you breed –
> Go bind your sons to exile
> To serve your captives' need;
> To wait in heavy harness,
> On fluttered folk and wild –
> Your new-caught, sullen peoples,
> Half-devil and half-child

At the beginning of the 20th century, racial pride became so intense in Europe that Europeans twice turned themselves against one another and, as a result, the whole world was plunged into two devastating wars because of the perceived racial superiority of the 'Aryan' Germans over other European nations.

In the 1960s, American civil rights campaigners, Martin Luther King Junior and Malcolm X, stirred American society with their demand for racial equality, albeit with different approaches. While the former followed a pacifist style in opposing racism, the latter used radical political campaign for racial equality. Martin Luther King's famous speech, 'When we let freedom ring, when we let it ring from every village and every hamlet, from every state and every city, we will be able to speed up that day when all of God's children, black men and white men, Jews and Gentiles, Protestants and Catholics, will be able to join hands and sing in the words of the old Negro spiritual, "Free at last, free at last. Thank God Almighty, we are free at last...",[17] has had a lasting influence on the fight for human equality in the West.

The establishment of the United Nations (UN) by the victorious allied powers of the Second World War gave some hope of universal human equality, but the arrogance of powerful countries dashed that hope within a few years. The formation of the present day European Union has, however, brought the European people under one umbrella. But this powerful 'North' does not seem to see the poorer and weaker 'South' in the same way they see themselves. Now, in the beginning of a new century, racial divide in many parts of the world is a menace to human society. In Britain the struggle to bring racial equality is still continuing.

Racism and Slavery

'Slavery was not born of racism; rather, racism was the consequence of slavery'.[18] Like racism, slavery is as old as civilisation itself. In most ancient empires the monster of racism and slavery existed simultaneously. The ancient Egyptians used slaves for building their monuments and pyramids. The Persians and the Greeks were no different. The Roman Empire had nearly 21 million slaves by about 50 CE.[19] However, slaves in ancient times were generally created due to war and taken from the vanquished nations. As such, slavery became an institution and an accepted norm borne out of warfare. Enslaved people were usually treated as inferior races. Although many of the cultural values and social customs of the enslaved people did infiltrate into the life of the victors, the latter were bent on destroying the culture and heritage of the former.

Slavery and the slave trade, linked with European colonialism, was different altogether and started during the sixteenth century when some European countries, especially Spain and Portugal, started occupying the two Americas. Britain and France followed suit. They turned their attention to the West Coast of Africa to capture the physically strong Africans and shipped them to their new-found colonies across the Atlantic. There was no war declared as such and those who were hunted down were not captives of any war either. This gave rise to the 'greatest crime in the world'; the trans-Atlantic slave trade. The forced emigration brought millions of Africans to America and the Caribbean. Enslaved Africans were often treated brutally by their captors and many of them died in the ships that carried them and their bodies were thrown into the Atlantic.

The black African slaves were regarded as uncivilised heathens, not proper human beings at all. They were sold to white masters whose main aim was to get as much work out of them for money and wealth. The treatment they suffered was inhuman, anything between threats and death. They were flogged, starved and grossly overworked in the American plantations. Some of them were even sadistically killed by being blown up with sticks of gun powder.[20] Attempted escape was punished by recapture and amputation in order to deter further attempts. Although there were some masters who treated their slaved in a relatively humane manner, slaves were dehumanised and desensitised with unprecedented barbarity. Often families were separated, and sold to different owners never to see each other again. The inhumanity of the slave trade has been encapsulated in many publications and has scarred the European conscience ever since.

Britain became the major European slave trading nation in the seventeenth and eighteenth centuries. However, the abolition movement to get the trade banned also started from Britain by the end of eighteenth century. An Abolition Society was formed in 1787, but faced violent objections from plantation owners and from those who believed that 'black savages' were meant to be natural slaves. The British Parliament finally banned the trade in 1807. It took a few more decades to enforce the ban in the trans-Atlantic route. Slavery was finally abolished in America after the Civil War (1861-65) when all slaves were freed. However, white supremacist groups such as the Ku Klux Klan, refused to accept this and kept on terrorising black people and those who supported them.

Racism and slavery originated from European colonialism, and has had a lasting impact in the course of modern history. Due to the brute force of the occupation the traditional life style and culture of the slaves and the colonised natives changed irreversibly. As these people gradually lost their root and heritage, so their confidence and ability to remain a strong social and political entity waned. They have now ended up as a marginalised, impoverished and disempowered people who are struggling to cope with life's many adversities. The story of the Aztecs, Incas and Indians of the American continent and the Maoris and Aborigines in Australasia is a tragedy for all humanity. Colonialism and racism have divided humanity ever since.

2. IMMIGRATION & RACE RELATIONS IN MODERN BRITAIN

Britain is not the homogeneous country it seems. Throughout its known history it has absorbed migrants including Romans, Angles, Saxons, Vikings, Danes, Jutes, Normans, Huguenots, Irish and Jews. Among these, the Irish and Jewish immigration to Britain is comparatively recent. The influx of Irish people started during the late eighteenth and early nineteenth centuries. By 1861 their numbers peaked.[21] The image of the Irish, racially and culturally inferior in popular British culture and often encapsulating in 'Irish jokes', 'was based not only on particular ideological constructions of the Irish but on a self-definition of Englishness or Anglo-Saxon culture'.[22]

On the other hand, the number of Jewish immigrants from Eastern Europe started to increase in the late nineteenth century. There was a contrast in British attitude regarding Jewish immigration *vis-à-vis* Irish immigration. The political reluctance to receive Jewish refugees because of anti-Semitism within British society was widespread.[23] 'Immigrant' and 'Jew' became synonymous because of extraordinary concerns for the social problems in London's East End which emerged roughly at the same time as the first great wave of immigration.[24]

However, all these white people of European extraction, including the Irish and the Jews, could easily make Britain their home because of their colour and cultural background. Once they became part of British society they were able to contribute to the new white British culture that we know today. As such, Britain feels at ease with white people from across the globe when they come here to visit or for settlement.

But, the twentieth century immigration of black and Asian people from Commonwealth countries created a new challenge for Britain, although the historical presence of black communities on the British Isles can be traced back over several centuries. By the end of the nineteenth century black seamen had settled in London and many port cities.[25]

During the inter-war period these 'Step Citizens'[26] and 'The Coolies of the Empire'[27] were linked with the social problems in the inner cities. 'Social decay was supposed to be connected with the presence of a 'Negro' population of Somalis, Arabs, West Indians, West Africans and so on, who constituted an almost insignificant percentage of the population of the sea-port cities.'[28]

Although they were British subjects, Indian seamen faced discriminatory treatment and during the slump in employment after the First World War Britain made further efforts to prevent them from settling in Britain. The competition for work resulted in racist violence against the Indian, Chinese, and Caribbean seamen in some port cities. Police sought to repatriate some of these seamen from Cardiff.[29] In the same way, the debate to control the immigration of 'coloured' people and repatriate those who had already settled in Britain continued after 1945. They were perceived as 'aliens' and a possible threat to the British way of life.[30]

Now, out of the 7.6% ethnic minority population in Britain (9% in England)[31] black and Asian people are largest in number. Over 11% of pupils in maintained primary and secondary schools in England and Wales are from minority ethnic groups. The immigration row with these 'coloured people' began in the early twentieth century and still continues to arouse debate in the political and social establishments today.

Post–War British Immigration Policies

During the Second World War, black workers and soldiers were instrumental in fighting for the British Empire. As a result, many of them arrived from the colonies to join the British army for the war effort. After the war there was a tremendous shortage of working age people in certain sectors of the British economy. Cheap labour was required. This gave rise to the ease of immigration regulations and the influx of black and Asian communities began. The arrival of the Empire *Windrush* in May 1948 with some 417 Jamaicans was a watershed in Black immigration in Britain. At the same time, because of the encouragement from the Labour government, thousands of Irish, Polish and other European people entered Britain to settle.

The contrast between the relatively liberal attitude towards the arrival of European workers and harsher attitude towards the 'coloured colonial workers' was evident in the attitudes of both the post-war Labour and Conservative governments. The Nationality Act (1948) and the Commonwealth Immigration Act (1962) attempted to address some of the intense debate within government departments and in public circles about the impact of black immigration on housing, the welfare state, crime and other social problems. The 1958 riots in Notting Hill in London and Nottingham paved in the development of 'racialised' politics in Britain.[32]

The Commonwealth Immigration Bill (1961), which became an act of Parliament the following year, legitimised the need for a halt on black immigration because of the difficulties of the host society in assimilating 'coloured immigrants', despite criticism from the Labour Party and sections of the press. The Act distinguished between the citizens of Britain and its colonies and citizens of independent Commonwealth countries. The main clauses sought to control the entry of black Commonwealth citizens into Britain. But, the Labour opposition shifted its direction and attempted to follow the Conservative footstep when it formed the government in 1964. In 1965 it published a white paper, *Immigration from the Commonwealth*, where they called for stricter immigration. This signalled a convergence of the policies of the Conservative and Labour Parties in favour of immigration controls.[33] Some people maintained that the white paper represented 'Little England' policy.[34]

During the 1964 parliamentary election campaign the immigration issue overshadowed the national political scene when Peter Griffiths of the Conservative Party claimed to defend the interests of the local white majority against the 'influx of immigrants'. The rhyme 'If you want a nigger neighbour, Vote Liberal or Labour' frequently used in favour of his candidacy was later defended by Mr. Griffiths as a 'manifestation of popular feeling' about immigration in the area. He refused to condemn those who used it.[35] 'For the first time in Britain, racism was openly injected into politics at the national level, and was seen to pay electoral dividends'.[36]

The arrival of East African Asians from 1965 onward sparked

the political debate surrounding immigration further and the debate reached its climax in 1967-68. As a response to a political campaign, the second Commonwealth Immigration Act came into effect in 1968 to control the flow of East African Asians, although most of them had British passports. The new law ruled that any citizen of Britain or its colonies with British passport would be subject to immigration control unless they or at least one parent or grandparent was born, adopted, naturalised or registered in Britain as a citizen of Britain or its colonies.[37]

During this period, one speech given by the Conservative politician Enoch Powell put the racial message in the forefront of the political agenda. In his infamously known 'rivers of blood' speech in Birmingham in April 1968, Powell sought to warn of the consequences of immigration that could lead to a 'total transformation to which there is no parallel in a thousand years of British history' and the danger of increasing racial tension in Britain, similar to America. Powell attempted to construct a grim picture of white Britons increasingly becoming 'isolated and strangers in their own country'.[38] In the ensuing political debate the immigration issue became linked with race. The Immigration Act (1971) and successive immigration rules issued by the Home Secretary to supplement the Act attempted to keep out black Commonwealth citizens as opposed to whites.[39] The 1981 British Nationality Act attempted to rationalise the 'existing racially discriminatory provisions of immigration law under the new clothing of British citizenship and the right of abode' in Britain.[40]

Race Relations Acts and Multiculturalism

In post-war Britain racial discrimination was legal. Employers, landlords and others could simply refuse to accept someone and state that 'no coloured' people were welcome. During the heightened political debate on race and immigration in the mid-1960s, the government attempted to address the issue by enacting the Race Relations Act (RRA) in 1965. The issue was not only race relations, but also of integration and assimilation into British society. However, in a speech to the National Committee for Commonwealth Immigrants on 23 May 1966 Roy Jenkins, the then Home Secretary, declared that he would 'define integration not as a flattening process of assimilation but as equal opportunity, accompanied by cultural diversity in an atmosphere of mutual tolerance'.[41] The RRA (1965) made it unlawful to discriminate on the grounds of race, colour, ethnic or national origin in public places, e.g., hotels, restaurants and swimming pools. A Race Relations Board was set up to receive complaints of discrimination.

The cause for good race relations was further enhanced when the Race Relations Act (1968) made discrimination in the area of employment, housing and the provision of goods and services unlawful. The Act had made it possible to bring cases of discrimination to court. Thus the race relation acts of the 1960's were gradually, albeit very slowly, leading Britain toward the notion of multiculturalism. At the same time, the trend of anti-racism among sections of society was also growing. This gave black communities some space and they formed alliances with some anti-racist groups. Although the opportunities were still limited, their traditions and cultures were beginning to be recognised. However, the stigma on black people and the assimilationist dimension of the race relations exercise kept undermining multiculturalism. Ignorance and prejudice remained as barriers.

The 1975 Home Office white paper, *Racial Discrimination*, acknowledged the need for stronger legislation and the 'need for a coherent and coordinated policy' on race relations to tackle 'more complex situations of accumulated disadvantages and the effects of past discrimination'.[42] This was a positive departure from the policies of previous government attitudes. In 1976 a new Race Relations Act came into existence. The RRA (1976) had a long-term impact on Britain's future race relations.

Multiculturalism was also taking a new shape as the 1976 Act covered indirect discrimination. At the same time, the Race Relations Board was replaced by the Commission for Racial Equality (CRE). The CRE was empowered with three main duties: work toward the elimination of discrimination; promote equality of opportunity and good race relations; and keep under review the working of the act and draw up proposals for amending it. The CRE was also given power to carry out monitoring of all these tasks.[43]

The RRA (1976), with the CRE at its helm and the Local Government Act (1966) that provided funds for promoting integration of New Commonwealth immigrants into British society, set the tone for more positive race relations in Britain. Later on, it was the Swann Committee that acknowledged the demand of and put forward the aspirations for multiculturalism in the educational field, i.e., in British schools.

A multicultural society such as ours would in fact function most effectively and harmoniously on the basis of pluralism which enables, expects and encourages members of all ethnic groups, both minority and majority, to participate fully in shaping society as a whole within a framework of commonly accepted values, practices and procedures, whilst also allowing and, where necessary, assisting the ethnic minority communities in maintaining their identities within this common framework.[44]

Multicultural Britain, according to Lord Swann, would be 'both socially cohesive and culturally diverse'.[45] The Swann

Committee's recommendations were received positively by minority communities.

Race-related Unrests and Government Responses

As in many other western countries, racial discrimination and racism have been a reality in modern Britain. Racism is still 'deeply embedded in white British society and eradicating it would take generations'.[46] The common features of racial discrimination are still blighting British society. Minority communities have become used to taking this for granted, as 'racial discrimination remains rampant in virtually all aspects of life in Britain'.[47]

Minority ethnic groups, however, did not always remain passive elements in British society. Rather, they have been an active political force over issues and policies that affect them, such as immigration, race relations, policing, etc. In modern Britain this has been violently reflected in some urban unrest. The riots in the early 1980s attracted national attention because of their serious nature. The April 1980 riot involving black residents and police in St. Paul's district of Bristol, the April 1981 riot between black youth and police in London's Brixton and the July 1981 riots in some cities including London, shook the country. But it was the events of April 1981 in Brixton that led the government to set up the Scarman Inquiry. The year 1985 also saw a number of riots in Birmingham (Handsworth), Tottenham, London (Brixton) and Liverpool. The unrest continued, albeit on a smaller scale, in 1986 and 1987.

Lord Scarman mentioned 'racial disadvantage' and 'immature and racially prejudiced actions' of some police officers 'particularly those below the level of the senior direction' in his inquiry.

> The evidence which I have received, the effect of which I have outlined ..., leaves no doubt in my mind that racial disadvantage is

a fact of current British life ... . Urgent action is needed if it is not to become an endemic, in-eradicable disease threatening the every survival of our society ... racial disadvantage and its nasty associate racial discrimination, have not yet been eliminated. They poison minds and attitudes; they are, as long as they remain, and will continue to be a potent factor of unrest.[48]

Some police officers of the force were guilty of 'ill-considered, immature and racially prejudiced actions ... in their dealings and on the streets with young black people. ... The police cannot rest on the argument that since they are a cross-section of society some officers are bound to be racially prejudiced. In this respect, as in others, the standards we apply to the police must be higher than the norms of behaviour prevalent in society as a whole'.[49]

There arose a heated debate among the politicians and in the media on the causes of the unrests. Were they related to the law and order issue and the difficulty of policing multi-racial inner city areas or to the poverty, unemployment, social deprivation, alienation and political marginality of the minority communities? Right wing media were, of course, bent on depicting a negative image of the black communities.

The incident that shook modern Britain and got wide national publicity was the cold-blooded race-motivated murder of a 19 year old black university student, Stephen Lawrence, on 22nd April 1993 in Eltham, south east London, by a gang of white youth. The Metropolitan Police mismanaged the case and their failure to apprehend the perpetrators of the crime gave a knee-jerk blow to their reputation as a public institution. A big race debate ensued and the new Labour government ordered a public inquiry under Sir William McPherson of Clunny. The McPherson report published in 1999 was scathing in its attack on the Metropolitan Police and exposed the racial discrimination, prejudice and violence which exist in society, and identified institutional racism –

'the collective failure of an organisation to provide an appropriate and professional service.' The report made 70 recommendations and prompted public services to take positive action to build an anti-racist society.

The serious disturbances in the summer of 2001 in some northern cities of England were the latest inner city unrests that put the necessity of 'community cohesion' in the forefront of the agenda. These disturbances between white and Asian youths in Oldham, Leeds, Burnley and Bradford were fuelled, it was accused, by the right wing British National Party (BNP). The extent of the damage shocked community leaders from all spectra. A number of reports on these disturbances blamed inner city deprivation, community segregation and youth criminality. The BNP took a dangerously one-sided view and blamed Muslims squarely for the trouble. The role of faith schools was questioned from some quarters in order to maintain that these schools were instrumental in creating community disharmony. However, it was easily established that almost all the youth from both sides of the trouble came from secular state schools. The disproportionate sentencing of Asian (Muslim) youth involved in the trouble became another point of controversy. The Labour Home Secretary, instead of helping cool down the frustration, used strong words to silence the critics.

A New Debate in Race Relations and Immigration Policy

In the 1980s due to the economic recession and rising levels of unemployment the Conservative government reinforced notions that the black British presence was a threat to Britain. The British Nationality Act (1981) reflected this attitude. The 1990s saw the surge of refugees and asylum seekers from some of the war ravaged countries, including Bosnia and Kosovo, to

Western European countries. Instead of recognising their plight Britain merely saw them as 'economic migrants' and as a result, an Asylum and Immigration Act (1996) was legislated. The Act curtailed many rights of immigrants and asylum seekers, e.g., income support, child benefits, and public housing. In spite of the concerns of Amnesty International and UNHCR, refugees were vilified by sections of the British press as the 'scum of the earth' and 'human sewage'.[50]

One act that has created anxiety particularly amongst the Muslim minority is the Terrorism Act (2000) which provides the authorities with the power to proscribe organisations engaged in international and domestic terrorism. As most of the proscribed organisations relate to Muslims, a few of which had been widely known to be engaged in freedom struggles in their own countries, this raised the fear of 'inadvertently reinforcing Islamophobia', according to the Muslim Council of Britain (MCB).

Tony Blair's Labour government appears to have taken a harder line on the immigration policy in their white paper, *Secure Borders, Safe Haven: Integration with Diversity in Modern Britain* published recently. It has raised a number of issues that ethnic minority leaders and human rights groups are finding difficult to accept. Many in minority communities have questioned the intrusive and patronising nature of the proposals, e.g., suggestions that British Asians should marry in the UK rather than in South Asia. The climate seems to be getting tenser on the debate. The sharpened hostility toward certain communities because of their race and religion has been the hallmark of misunderstanding and intolerance in the race and community relations debate in the beginning of the new century. This seems to be giving ammunition to the openly racist British National Party (BNP) who are making inroads in local politics by capitalising mainly on the wave of Islamophobia.

With the publication of the McPherson Report (1999), the summer disturbances of 2001 in northern England, the September 11 atrocities in the US and the upsurge in the debate surrounding asylum seekers, race has once again returned to the centre stage of debate in British politics. The recommendations from of McPherson Report and the strong feelings surrounding issues linked with Muslims have aroused negative feelings towards multiculturalism in some quarter of British policy.

In the present phase, the attack on multiculturalism has been coming from those who generally blame South Asians and specifically Muslims for their resilience in keeping their religious identity. Those who spearhead this attack have the erroneous idea that Muslims are a monolithic people who are unwilling to be part of the wider British society. What is otherwise a democratic right of any community in a pluralist society, e.g., parental choice of schools, school dress, language, dietary restrictions, opting out in certain curriculum areas, etc, is seen as intransigence by this powerful section. It is sometimes forgotten that issues like those mentioned above are not exclusive to Muslims alone and, in fact, many communities are making similar demands. The insensitivity of a section of the media is contributing toward increasing tensions in community relations and probably exacerbating racism of a religious nature.

3. BARRIERS TO RACE RELATIONS

'This is a white man's country, and I want it to remain so.'[51] It is thoughts such as these that always create tension among communities. Any outburst of racial tension has, of course, multiple reasons - historical, socio-economic and educational. Ignorance, an arrogant attitude, lack of respect for others and fear give rise to racism which is inherent in many societies. Racism is determined by the beliefs and actions of individuals and institutions, often exacerbated by policies and laws of the state. It can be overt, involving individual acts of oppression against other individual or racial groups. It may also be covert and institutional; marginalising racial groups that are thought to be different or inferior. Racism is most likely to appear when the differences between groups are ostentatious, as in differences of language, physical appearance, or cultural expressions. It consists of conduct, words or practices which give advantage or disadvantage to people because of their colour, culture or ethnic origin. In its more subtle form it is as damaging as in its overt form.

Barriers to race relations are erected by both individuals and by institutional racism. This arises due to the appearance of people's sense of superiority over others. In the beginning of human creation, according to the Abrahamic religions, the devil thought himself superior to Adam because he was made of fire whilst Adam was of clay.[52] This made the devil haughty and he failed to acknowledge the worth of Adam.

Racism gives rise to discrimination. 'Institutional discrimination' consists of the collective failure of an organisation to provide an appropriate and professional service to people because of their diversity or differences. It can be seen or detected in processes, attitudes and behaviours that amount to discrimination through unwitting prejudices, ignorance, thoughtlessness and stereotyping which disadvantage individuals and groups. Some groups face more racism than others for historic, amongst other, reasons. 'Members of the ethnic minorities as a whole, in particular Blacks and Asians, experience a number of social disadvantages to a greater extent than other groups'.[53]

Individual attitudes toward people of different background contribute towards race relationships, but discrimination and racism can be seen in institutional policies, practices, procedures and processes. Ineffective consultation, lack of monitoring and reviewing of policies and their impact on specific groups, lack of sensitivity toward minority ethnic groups, lack of capacity in certain ethnic groups, discriminatory practice in recruitment and promotion of minority ethnic staff, informal cliques within organisations, stereotyping, lack of openness to the personal values and beliefs of others and the use of inappropriate language – are some of the causes of institutional racism.

In almost all minority communities there are some who choose self-segregation for fear of assimilation in the cultural melting pot of mainstream society and there are others who just give in to the demands of the dominant cultural trend. Many communities, in spite of having their distinctive culture or proud heritage, feel disadvantaged in the new environment. If the dominant society, instead of accepting them with openness, shows prejudice or hostility the minority suffer in employment, education and other areas of life. Their lack of confidence tends to make them more excluded and marginalised.

Vital public service organisations such as the police and education authorities on the one hand, and media establishments on the other, can exacerbate or reduce these barriers through their policies and actions.

Race Relations and Policing

The police are the most important instrument for maintaining law and order in society and are generally the first point of contact for most people within the criminal justice system. As a result, the attitude and behaviour of the police, in dealing with members of ethnic communities, is key to establishing equality before the law. Minority communities settling in a culturally dominant and often hostile social environment need understanding and, at times, protection from the establishment, especially from those responsible for maintaining law and order. But time and again the police have shown insensitivity and, in some cases, hostility to minority communities. Although, over the last few decades, the police have been trying to build bridges with minority communities there is still a serious lack of trust.

When racism, in the form of racial prejudice and harassment, is widespread in a society it is obvious that the police force cannot remain unaffected, as they are a part of society. Sad though it is, some police officers tend to hide their inaction behind this social reality. Some of Britain's police forces have themselves acknowl-

edged their weaknesses of insensitive or racially-motivated policing long before the McPherson Report in 1999. Some have lined
up to say so after the report.

After the 1985 riots a number of initiatives were introduced
by the police, e.g., measures to increase recruitment of police officers from the minority communities, improved training for police recruits, the formation of community relations and policies for
tackling racial harassment.[54] Unfortunately, police forces could not
achieve their target and as a result there is still a big confidence gap
in all this. Minority communities still feel that the police are on
the 'other side'.

Many smaller communities suffer badly because of their lack
of representation in public life. In 1990 less than 1% of police officers in the UK were from minority ethnic group. Things were
not any better in other local and central government employment.
In spite of all the rhetoric this has not changed much in the last
decade. The extent of police harassment faced by the minority
communities has created resentment, especially amongst black and
Asian young men. According to The National Association for the
Care and Resettlement of Offenders (NACRO) black people are
more likely to be stopped and searched by the police, to be prose-
cuted and to receive a prison sentence. Now there is a strong feeling that Asians, especially Muslim youth, are catching up in this.
The high proportion of Muslim prisoners in British jails is a cause
of concern for all.

Perpetrators of racial violence and harassment are from all
sections of the wider community and the police have a duty to
remain fair in their attitudes and actions. They are specifically
blamed because of their sensitive tasks.[55] Research shows that one
fifth to a quarter of white people admitted they harboured racial
prejudices against minorities.[56] About half of the respondents who

had reported being subjected to some form of racial harassment were dissatisfied with the police response. According to the survey, victims of racism felt the police had acted in a manner which was unreasonable and which they interpreted as being racist or, at best, in implicit sympathy with the perpetrators. 'The police were perceived to have shown a lack of interest or indifference towards addressing the problem even though the incident constituted a criminal assault'.[57] With strong feelings in minority communities about the police, the latter have a big task in convincing the former of their fairness. The onus of building trust is generally on the strong and powerful people within the society.

Race Relations in School

Education is at the heart of sustaining the values and norms of a society. Quality education produces capable people in all spheres of life so that they can effectively take over the responsibility of their predecessors to run the machineries of the country. Developed countries are generally able to harness the potentials of their younger generation through education and train them to fulfil their citizenship responsibilities. When a society becomes inclusive, its education also becomes inclusive and vice versa. Through inclusive education a country tries hard to ensure that no section of its populace misses out on an education for whatever reason - disability, economic and social disadvantage, racism, religious discrimination, etc.

Historically, the education curriculum in most western countries was Euro-centric. This has remained so even though most European countries have become pluralist. In a plural and multicultural society education has to reflect the culture and history of all people so that children grow with informed knowledge about others, including their own. If this is absent in any education system children miss out on the richness of other cultures. There have been attempts to redress the situation in some areas of the curriculum, but the progress is by and large very slow. Given the overall not-so-friendly racial situation and immigration row in Britain, most Afro-Caribbean boys under-perform due to institutional racism.[58] Raising the achievement of Bangladeshi and Pakistani boys has also become a matter of concern recently.

Bangladeshi and Pakistani children, most of whom are Muslims, achieve low grades in GCSE exams.[59] Few of them continue onto further education.[60] As a result of underachieving in education and other socio-economic factors, unemployment rates amongst them, on the basis of ILO definition, is high61 (27% in 1995, i.e., three to four times higher than that of the white population). The latest major piece of research carried out by the Policy Studies Institute (PSI) paints a depressing picture of these two communities in Britain.[62] The occasional negative portrayal of the *hijab* and beard for Muslim children and the turban for Sikh children in schools, displays the lack of confidence in multi-culturalism in some quarters. The exclusion figures among black secondary pupils are disproportionately high compared to others. Many people, including the current chairman of the CRE, Trevor Philips, criticise schools for failing black pupils. Afro-Caribbean pupils achieve a lot less compared to white pupils in terms of five A* - C grades at GCSE level.

Although Section 11 of the Local Government Act (1966), which has now become the Ethnic Minorities Achievement Grant (EMAG), helped LEAs to employ extra staff from new Commonwealth countries for the teaching of English as a second language, this has not helped much in the inclusion process in schools. Many children from minority communities still experience difficulties arising from cultural differences, including those of language, religion and customs.[63]

The race debate in education came to prominence in the mid 1980s as a result of attempts by some Labour LEAs to implement anti-racist policies. The controversy surrounding Bradford head teacher Ray Honeyford became a national one when he criticised multicultural education in favour of integration. The affair had its ramification on the education debate for a long time.[64]

Racism can take many forms in schools. In the higher level, it gives rise to aggressive conflict through name-calling and other verbal taunts, leading to bullying and physical violence. In the lower level, the pattern can be observed in one or more of the following:[65]

Exclusion from friendship groups

Exclusion from activities

Racialised gossip

Racialisation of romance relationships

The policy makers and the practitioners in the field of education should address the need to making the curriculum accessible and sensitive to all on the one hand, and provide education in an anti-racist and safe environment on the other. That was the whole purpose of multicultural and comprehensive education for the past few decades. With a lot of missing elements in it, the success was very limited. With the recent emphasis on 'inclusion' in the educational world the need for genuine inclusion of all the communities is ever greater.

Race Relations and the Media

Media, broadcasting and the press, are proving ever more important in creating community relationship in a society. In modern society the mass media plays a vital role in leading opinions, directing national debates and building bridges between people. Conversely, they can play a destructive role in creating negative stereotypes of minority groups, their cultures and history, and thus dividing a society. They can stigmatise minority communities by linking them with activities such as crime, drug addiction and, in recent times, terrorism. The media reporting of issues such as immigration and asylum seeking, street crime and gun culture linked with particular groups, can put those communities in difficulties. The media can either highlight discrimination and inequality in a society in order to create awareness for their alleviation or can cause discrimination and inequality by demonising certain communities.

The media industry in the western countries is generally run by tycoons and some of them wield tremendous influence through their global networks. Governments, generally, do not directly run media, but because of their political muscles their views are generally taken on board by the media industry. There are formal and informal relationships between the media and the government. Government information is circulated through press releases and briefings. Sometimes politicians want to directly influence media. In post-September 11 America the media industry has generally tuned to the federal government line. This may have a ripple effect in other western countries.

The police and the media can enhance community harmony by their responsible dealings on community issues or fuel the flame of racial prejudice by linking race and crime in the country. When sensitive information is not dealt properly it can create social tension and hatred. Enoch Powell's assertion of mugging as a black crime in 1976 were taken on board by two right wing tabloids, the *Daily Mail* and the *Sun*, and put the black community on the receiving end. The ideological image of young blacks mugging and committing other forms of youth crimes has shifted the political language and provided the basis of policing for the last few decades, especially in the inner cities.

There now seems to be a trend within a section of the media to demonise Asian Muslim youth for their alleged failure to assimilate into the mainstream society. They are generally being accused of holding extreme views. Like the linking of black people with crime in the past decades Muslims are now facing the similar stereotype of being extremist. The disproportionate media coverage of the heavy-handed raid on Finsbury Park mosque by the police in January 2003 and the highly publicised threat of terrorism on the Muslim festival of Eid on 11th February in the same year created consternation among Muslims. Within a few months the BBC, which is run by the license fees from common people, went ahead with screening of their damaging fictional drama 'Spooks' in spite of massive opposition from the community.

Media denigration puts a community in serious disadvantage in the public eye. For communities that are already suffering from economic and social deprivation this fosters further alienation and frustration. As such, people of all ethnic and religious backgrounds deserve better treatment from the media.

4. THE CHALLENGE OF PLURALISM

Anti-Racism Movement and its Impact

'[Their] contribution is incredibly wide and varied – from the economy, politics, public service and the law, medicine, the arts and even our cooking. It is a contribution which today forms part of our national identity, and it adds immeasurably to the richness and creativity of modern Britain.[66]

Comments like the one mentioned above by Prince Charles acknowledge the contributions minority communities have made to Britain over the decades. However, the history of the anti-racism struggle in Britain is as long as the struggle by the immigrant communities to have their rightful place in society. People from Commonwealth countries saw this as a challenge in which many people from the indigenous society joined ranks. Like the anti-slavery movement in the eighteenth century, the post-War anti-racist movement also took a global shape with concerted campaigns in America, South Africa, Britain and other places. In Britain, racism and racial discrimination was confronted in the following ways.

- Through public awareness campaigns which were boosted by the global antipathy for racism. Fighting racism and xenophobia became the widely accepted issues across the world through seminars and symposia by the UN and other bodies. They gradually created an atmosphere of revulsion against open racism in society. Many unsung heroes put their lives at risk in this campaign;

- Through legislation and enactment of legal measures outlawing discriminatory acts. Although legislation alone does not produce change in everyday discriminatory practices in employment and service provision, such measures give the legal backing to defend the victims of racism.

- Through political strategy against discrimination or development of positive action by central and local governments. This creates an environment where open racism is curtailed and perpetrators are politically challenged.

Successive British governments, however, took an ambivalent attitude toward this anti-racist measures and failed to sufficiently empower organisations such as the Commission for Racial Equality (CRE) in bringing about fundamental changes in race relations. Since 1976, Britain has had a lack of serious cohesive plans with governments generally sticking to piecemeal actions rather than co-ordinated public policies to eradicate racism from society. The proactive initiative found in controlling immigration and asylum seeking was not found in working for anti-discrimination legislation. Questions now arise as to whether this lack of seriousness is inherent in social policies within a capitalistic western society, and whether reform policies are simply symbolic in nature. On the other hand, there is a tendency in the popular media to blame the minority communities themselves - or the race relations industry - rather than racism itself as the source of problems.

In spite of this lack of serious progress in this field, anti-racism has strengthened its root in the public mind. Most people have become vocal against overt racism and developed a revulsion against covert racism. However, it is observed that most anti-racism campaigns had been waged by the liberal, leftist or radical sections of society. While liberals want to remove misunderstanding through, say, multicultural education in schools and through laws; radicals stress that robust political and structural measures are required because of the deep-rooted culture of racism in society. As long as the trend of anti-racist feeling does not become a part of the social and political culture of society racism would remain a serious issue in Britain.

The Changing Nature of Multiculturalism

The changing nature of Britain's ethnic diversity was initially guided by debates on the immigration of minority communities into Britain. Estimates of the rate of immigration and the size of the minority ethnic population were used by the opponents and proponents of immigration controls to devise policies on race relations. It was generally felt that migrants from the Commonwealth, if the number was large, were a potential problem. Many thought that the solution lay in their assimilation into the dominant society through which migrants would no longer look like 'strangers'. 'A consequence of this immigration-led focus of government policy was that, until recently, most official estimates of the size of the minority ethnic population were based on data about the place of birth of those born outside the UK'.[67]

However, with the increasing number of second and third generation people within the migrant communities from the Commonwealth the debate gradually shifted towards the issue of ethnicity. During the prolonged debate on ethnicity in the 1980s the following schema was finally accepted for the 1991 Census for the classification of racial groups in Britain:

White UK
Black Caribbean
Black African
Black Other (please describe)
Indian
Pakistani
Bangladeshi
Chinese
Any other

The CRE adopted these categories for ethnic monitoring purposes. Many education authorities added two sub-classifications
(white European and white other) to describe white people in
their school populations. The 2001 Census has updated the classification slightly and the schema was as follows;

White
British
Irish
Any other White background

Mixed
White and Black Caribbean
White and Black African
White and Asian
Any other Mixed background

Asian or Asian British
Indian
Pakistani
Bangladeshi
Any other Asian background

Black or Black British
Caribbean
African
Any other Black background

Chinese or other ethnic group
Chinese
Any other

Toward a Genuine Pluralism

Britain, in the beginning of the 21st century, has come a long way from the Britain of the 1960s. Its landscape and demography have changed irreversibly over the decades. Britain can now celebrate its diversity with people from around the globe who are contributing to the formation of a pluralist society. Pluralism has taken a natural form in major cities of the British Isle. 1 in 13 people in Britain (7.6% of the population, about 4.5 million people) are now from minority ethnic communities and in England this has risen from 6% in 1991 to 9% in 2001. The 2001 Census revealed that black and Asian people comprised 60.6% of the population in one London borough (Newham) and 54.7% in another (Brent). Sixteen other London boroughs had black and Asian minorities that accounted for a quarter or more of the population. Leicester became the first city-wide authority with the largest proportion of non-whites (more than one third of the population) followed by Slough (36.3%), Birmingham (29.6%) and Luton (28.1%).[68] Britain has indeed become the microcosm of the world.

Can Britain eradicate racial inequality from its society? The government's announcement in May 2002 to bring together the Equal Opportunities Commission, the Commission for Racial Equality and Disability Rights Commission into a single equality body gives the signal that it intends to enhance Britain's equality framework. Whether merging these bodies brings the intended equality remains to be seen. It seems that a long hard battle lies ahead. Figures from the 2001 Census on racial inequality do not, however, give an encouraging picture. In its m*ain headline, Britain*

Today: A Nation Still Failing its Ethnic Minorities, on 8th May 2003 the Independent mentioned that 'while England is becoming more multi-cultural, second and even third generation immigrants are still among the most deprived in society.' The deprivation and inequality are across the board, in all areas of life. 'The proportion of Muslim children living in overcrowded accommodation is more than three times the national average, that they are twice as likely to be in a house with no central heating and children from Pakistani and Bangladeshi families suffer twice as much ill health as their white counterparts', it said. A lot of hard work needs to be done to overcome this and bring a minimum level of racial equality in coming years.

Can Britain catch its racism bull by the horn? There again seems to be a lot of challenges ahead. Even ten years after the brutal racist murder of Stephen Lawrence, Commander Cressida Dick, Head of Diversity Directorate of the Metropolitan Police, acknowledged that 'while great strides have been made to tackle organisational racism, it is unlikely ever to be completely eradicated, as race hate is a problem for society as a whole.'[69] With the international situation getting more complex the challenges toward eradicating racism in Britain remain high.

However, there is only one choice for all to work in this field – to struggle together towards building and sustaining a pluralist society in modern Britain. It is a collective endeavour for both the majority and minority communities. In order to achieve that goal individuals and institutions need understanding, tolerance and the recognition of every human being, irrespective of background. Minority communities deserve respect and recognition in the same way the majority community does. All people in society should be accepted with equal worth so that they can speak for themselves and participate in all decisions affecting their lives. 'Respect and recognition go beyond equal opportunity and call for a profound change in white society's attitudes to ethnic minorities'.[70] One guideline from the Qur'an seems uniquely relevant in this regard:

> *'O you who believe! Let not some men among you laugh at others; it may be that the latter are better than the former. Nor let some women laugh at others; it may be that the latter are better than the former. Nor defame nor be sarcastic to each other; nor call each other by (offensive) nicknames.*[71]

5. RELIGION, FAITH, & COMMUNITY

Religion

Religion has occupied a central role in life since the beginning of human creation and still remains so. Religion consists of beliefs, actions and institutions which assume the existence of supernatural entities with powers of action or impersonal powers or processes possessed of moral purpose.[72]

Whether religion is a belief in some higher authority, divine being, or a set of rituals or practices, it has been a big debate among people of various religious backgrounds. To anthropologists it entails 'beliefs and practice in communities'. To sociologists religious ideas relates to society that give individuals a sense of purpose and meaning. Historians, however, describe it in terms of events resulting from beliefs. Theologians, on the other hand, are concerned with beliefs themselves and they study religions from scriptures and interpretation of the scriptures.

While theologians study religion from inside assuming that it is the ultimate truth related to the world and the cosmos, academicians study it from outside and in a neutral and non-committal manner. Whereas the interpretation of religious scriptures by theologians gives rise to various schools of thought and sectarian divisions, academic study of religion concentrates only on its visible aspects and people's religious experiences.

Social scientists identify religions in terms of their functions i.e., 'what religion does'. Religions, generally provided – or attempted to provide – solutions to problems or answered questions in the past. But, as societies have become more complex, many of the problems and questions in real life are now treated as being 'secular' rather than 'religious' dilemmas. In modern societies, religions are thus becoming more sidelined, although their influence is increasing now.

Philosophers and scholars tend to see religion in their own image. For example, Marx explained it in economic terms, Freud in sexual terms and post-Darwinian anthropologists in terms of evolution. The scriptures of the three Abrahamic religions, i.e., Judaism, Christianity and Islam, maintain that religion comes from the same God and is as old as human history. According to Islam, the first man, Adam, was himself a Prophet who taught his progeny how to live as true servants of God on earth. From Adam to Muhammad, all the Prophets were given exactly the same message of truth and guidance, albeit within the context of their time and space. God only accepts a religion where human beings surrender to His will.[73] Islam teaches human beings about the purpose of their creation, their existence and their ultimate destiny vis a vis their place amongst other creatures on earth.

Faith

Although faith and religion are often used interchangeably for practical purposes, faith is a generalised term and is an attitude or idea of the 'self', including one's will and intellect, toward a person or a divine being. It is the inner attitude, conviction or trust relating a human being to a Supreme Being or God. Faith includes religious belief and often goes far beyond it. It is also the personal feeling that gives stability and meaning in many people's life.

Faith is linked with good works in all religious traditions. In the Abrahamic tradition, faith evokes a covenant between man and God. Whether the demands of faith are compatible with those of reason is another question, one that is related with the wisdom of religious hierarchy. In medieval Europe this created a friction between priests representing the church and rational humanists or scientists. This continued for a long time with the triumph of rationalism over the Church.

In Islam, faith (Arabic: *Iman*) is the belief in the unseen,[74] which incorporates three essential aspects: *Tawheed* (the oneness of God), *Risalah* (Prophethood) and *Akhirah* (life after death). These beliefs determine a Muslim's life from cradle to grave and from mundane affairs to the highest intellectual aspect of life. A person's faith is only by the will of God.[75] It is similar to Christian belief in that it is a gift from God.[76] Islam identifies people from others who have no faith or confusion about faith. Faith is the primary element in Islam and is integrally linked with action (Arabic: *Amal*). Faith and action are dependent on knowledge and understanding. It is due to this reason that knowledge is essential in Islam.

Community

A community is made up of people who are grouped together by their common interests.[77] The bond between people in a community could be due to ethnicity, residence, social status, activities, etc. A community could be made up of smaller communities as well, a community of communities, as in the case of the Muslim community or *ummah*. Human beings are interlinked by relationships with others in the community.

Communities can emerge for a short-term objective, e.g., campaign groups, and long-term historical purposes, e.g., faith communities. Individuals may belong to many different communities at the same time and their allegiances can fluctuate.[78] 'Community' refers accurately to a strong sense of group identity.[79] Communities settling in a new environment often struggle to maintain this solidarity. As cultures and subcultures struggle to survive in an alien social environment, communities adapt and learn from others. They cannot remain cut off from the rest of the society.

Community development or regeneration is the process of growing and building capacity in the context of a community's existence and empowering it with the skills to move forward. In order to do this individuals and groups need to network, share knowledge and skills, learn from each others experiences and develop partnerships with other communities and agencies. In a pluralist society, communities need internal capacity building to sustain and progress. Although members feel proud in being associated with their own community they do not feel excluded from mainstream society in a pluralist set up. They do not feel socially and economically vulnerable.

6. MILESTONES IN THE RELIGIOUS HISTORY OF BRITAIN

Although Britain's religious history goes back to the fourth millennium BC[80] with Stonehenge as one of the ceremonial monuments of the pre-Roman period, Britain's religious history took a definitive direction from its Roman legacy. It started with the historic conversion of the Roman Emperor Constantine (280-337 CE) to Christianity. As Christianity became the state religion, he effectively became the head of the religion. With newly found state power the church was able to resolve its century-old theological disputes by legal rather than philosophical means. At the Council of Nicaea in 325 CE, headed by Emperor Constantine, Christian orthodoxy was finally defined with the doctrine of Trinity and the adoption of four canonical gospels as the Scriptures. It also institutionalised punishment for 'heresy', i.e., any one who would not conform to the orthodoxy was liable to be punished.

With this new development in the Roman Empire, Christianity gradually replaced old religious beliefs or paganism in Britain. By the end of the fifth century, Christianity established itself and provided a sense of security and continuity on the British Isle.[81] In the Medieval Ages no area of British social life was void of the influence of Christianity and no important social event went without the involvement of the Church. The medieval church was linked to either supra-national entities such as the Holy Roman Empire or to the emerging nation-state and it maintained its dominant influence on the lives of ordinary people through the cathedral and through the ties of parish church with the local community.[82] Since the beginning of the second millennium a number of historical events shaped the course of British religious and political history. They were the Crusades, the Renaissance and Reformation and the activities of Christian missionaries in the colonies.

The Legacy of the Crusades

No event in history has had more impact on the European psyche than the Crusades or organised military expeditions by European Christians to drive Muslims from the Holy Lands, including Jerusalem. The word 'Crusade', derived from the Latin 'crux' for cross, which the Crusaders wore on their tunics.[83] Jerusalem, the Holy City of the three Abrahamic religions, was the central focus of most of the Crusades. Under Muslim rule it was an open city for all three religions; Muslim tolerance of the other religious people was exemplary.[84] However, it was an irony that Christianity, known as a religion of love, was used by the Crusaders to spill the blood of not only Muslims in the Holy Land, but also of Jews and Eastern Christians.

Historians record eight Crusades spanning from the eleventh to the fourteenth century. Some are renowned in history. The first Crusade (1096-99CE) initiated by Pope Urban II created havoc in many cities across Palestine and ended with a victory bloodbath in Jerusalem. Tens of thousands of Muslims and Jews were slaughtered.[85] After this terrible event Muslims began to consolidate their power in Palestine and, in the second Crusade, retook Edessa in 1144 CE. However, they lost control of Lisbon in Portugal in 1147 CE. In the following decades Muslims gained territories in Palestine and under Saladin (Sultan Salahuddin Ayyubi) retook Jerusalem in 1187 CE. Saladin became known as a humane and intelligent ruler. He did not allow his army to sack the city, in order to prevent unnecessary casualties.[86] The Crusaders' savagery with their opponents, including Christians, on their way back tarnished their image. Conversely, Saladin's magnanimity with the Christians and Crusaders made him a legend.[87]

The third Crusade came as a response to this continuous Muslim success and European kings, including Richard I of England, took part in it. The fourth Crusade did not reach Jerusalem, but the Crusaders plundered the Christian city of Constantinople in 1204 CE. The Children's Crusade of 1212 CE resulted in twenty thousand children being sold as slaves in Egypt.[88]

The Crusades did not stop even after the Crusaders were driven out of the Holy Land in 1291 CE, but directed their war against the Ottoman advance in the Balkans. The confrontation between the two great religions continued. However, through this encounter or interaction one underlying event was taking shape in Europe that changed the history of humankind irreversibly and that was the liberation of the European mind from the orthodox Christian establishment. Europe gained much from the richness of Muslim intellectual creativity and social values. This helped the Europeans in initiating an intellectual reawakening which later paved the way for the Renaissance and Reformation.

The Renaissance and Reformation

In the Middle Ages European thought was confined to the monasteries and rigidly controlled by the Church.[89] Corruption was rife in the Church establishment and popes had more interest in politics and wealth than the spiritual well being of people. There were increasing protests against the power, authority and corruption of the popes during the fourteenth and fifteenth centuries. The protesters became known as Protestants, and Protestant churches started to appear in western Europe, including Britain, during that period. Wars broke out in many parts of Europe. The Church ultimately divided into two, Catholicism and Protestantism.

Against this backdrop emerged the liberal intellectual revival of the Renaissance, which was given a tremendous boost by the invention of the printing press in 1451 CE. The contribution of Muslim scholars and the ancient Greeks – via texts translated by Arab scholars into Latin - fuelled the Renaissance. A priest in Florence established a Platonic Academy and published Plato's ideas in Latin with commentaries.

As Rome was the centre of Christianity, a number of Italian philosophers, priests and politicians of started challenging Christian orthodoxy in its heartland. The Renaissance, with its capacity for reason, opened the lid of the human mind and created an avalanche of human experiment on self-investigation, discovery and understanding. The humanist concept of life promoted by the Renaissance started empowering the European mind. During the sixteenth and seventeenth centuries, the fire of the Renaissance spread to England, France and some other European countries.

The history of the Reformation goes back to 1517 CE when the German priest Martin Luther first raised his complaint against the excesses of the medieval church. It was more than a theological disagreement. It raised a voice of simmering social, political and economic discontent in western Europe. The Reformation process, mainly in the north-west of Europe, gave rise to counter-reformation in the south. This led to civil wars in parts of Europe. In 1542 CE the Universal Inquisition was set up by Pope Paul III to seek out Protestants to recant. Muslims and Jews became targets of the Spanish Inquisition during this period. Many people were burnt to death and scientists and philosophers were persecuted. The massacre of French Protestants (Huguenots) in 1562 CE was a particularly cruel episode. In England, the Reformation led to the political breakaway of the Anglican Church from the Catholicism domain under Henry VIII.

The Renaissance and Reformation had a profound influence on European thought that led to massive changes in European so-cieties. Although it took hundreds of years to change Europe, the ramifications were far reaching. It encouraged individualism, the nascent concepts of human rights and, above all, the humanist concept of life with the confidence of power of men and women to govern their own affairs.[90]

By stressing rights and responsibilities of individuals and the equality of all in the eyes of God, the Renaissance and Reformation brought an end to feudalism and gave birth to democracy in Europe. However, although the target of the Reformation was to reform the Church, it fragmented Christendom. During, the eigh-teenth and nineteenth centuries, religious sects within Christianity (e.g., Presbyterians, Quakers, Baptists and Methodists) emerged. However, some of them have gradually taking the form of de-nominations.

Christian Missions and the Impact

Christianity in the Middle Ages was largely a European religion with the exception of Christians in some parts of the Middle East.

Europe's trade with the rest of the world and its colonial enterprises aroused the missionary zeal in many Europeans to convert native people in the weaker countries to Christianity. Portugal represented the arrival of a new power and its faith.[91] The fifteenth and sixteenth century Portuguese, Spanish, and French expansion encouraged Catholic missions to the Americas and Asia. With the British colonial expansion in the nineteenth century British Protestant missions spread out in the world.

These missions made Christianity a world religion by the end of the nineteenth century. The attempts by various Christian churches to win over poorer people in the colonised countries remained a contentious issue for centuries. Many who struggled to defend their religion and culture from European aggression considered this a further humiliation to their dignity, 'adding insult to their injury'. Hinduism, Buddhism, Confucianism and in particular Islam strongly resisted Christianity. The battle was as much political and cultural as it was religious.

From the Christian point of view the missionaries were ordained by God to show human beings the way to 'salvation through Jesus Christ'. Missionaries did, however, do some important medical and educational works in impoverished communities. The conversion agenda was generally not successful. In a number of cases, however, particularly in relation to the African religions, there were some successes.

The fact that the British Anglican church now has over seventy million people around the world is a testimony to this. The post-colonial European churches tried to modify their approach and attempted to work with the sensitivities of other religious people. In Britain, churches of various denominations have realised the importance of working with other religious groups. This helped in the gradual establishment of dialogue between various faith communities in order to promote religious coexistence. The emergence of national and local interfaith bodies is now a socio-political reality in Britain.

7. RELIGIOUS PLURALISM IN BRITAIN

Religious 'Belonging'

A pluralist and democratic society prides freedom of expression and individual rights to practice religion, until it violates others rights. 'Everyone is entitled to believe what they want'. It is also expected that people do not become judgmental about other people's belief. Europe had to fight for this freedom of religious belief and it won it with a heavy cost. Although Church and state are separate, religion still has influence in one's life. How far it affects the public life is, of course, a matter of debate. If religious practice is a pointer of people's religiosity then most European countries have developed a reluctance for it. However, still most people are ready to display their religious affinity. A survey conducted about a decade ago showed the following figures;[92]

Non-Church going Christians	55%
Atheists/Agnostics	27%
Church going Christians	10%
Religious non-Christians	8%

These figures do not represent the exact nature of religious commitment of Christians, as it is widely known that some Church-goers, including clergy and ministers, have a very secular world view. On the other hand, many Christians who never attend church are ready to affirm their traditional Christian faith. They also want their children to be taught those beliefs in schools. The existence of, and undiminished support for, many faith schools confirms this.

In the latter part of the twentieth century Christians in Britain have gradually shown more apathy towards religious practices, e.g., baptism, marriage, ordination, Sunday attendance. However, during this time, Britain has also seen a revival of faith activities with the Independent, Afro-Caribbean and Pentecostal Churches, the Sects, the New Religious Movements and other non-Christian religions coming in the picture. Among them Jehova's Witnesses, Mormons, Moonies and the Hare Krishna movement have expanded rapidly. While the New Free Churches are evangelical in nature, cults and New Religious Movements are colourful in their presentation. Some of these groups get wide mainstream media coverage. The immigration after 1947 from South Asia and after 1948 from the Caribbean saw a huge influx of people with diverse religious affiliation into Britain. As Afro-Caribbean people found endemic racism in British society they established their own Churches, although most immigrants from Jamaica were Christians and a large section of them were Church-goers. Black Churches in Britain thus represent racial and religious segregation as well.

Buddhism, Islam, Hinduism and Sikhism are now flourishing in Britain. Although the Immigration Act (1962) put some control in the process of immigration from Commonwealth countries these religions continued to flourish due to higher birth rates amongst their followers and arrival of co-religionist family members. Islam and Buddhism have also experienced growth due to conversions. Judaism although it has a longer history in Britain and is better integrated with the structures of power in Britain lost people because of non-practice, emigration and intermarriage. Their number has significantly decreased in the last few decades. However, like the Christian Church they have well-established institutions. The Board of Deputies of British Jews has more than 150 years of history and the Chief Rabbi is a peer in the House of Lords. They are well-represented in parliament, government, business, media and other sectors of public life. Anti-Semitism was common in the 1930s, but negligible now.

In the last two decades Britain's religious diversity has given rise to major activities due to the rising trend of using faith as an identity amongst many people, and interfaith work between major religions in the country. Religion is now gradually wielding more influence in public life of modern Britain. In the 1980s, the Church of England, under Robert Runcie, raised voices of dissent against some of the policies of the then prime minister, Margaret Thatcher. This raised the profile of religion in general and Christianity in particular.

Church attendance might be dwindling, but more people are now ready to identify with Christianity. The comparative figures of people 'belonging' to Christianity (55.6% in 1979 to 71.6% in 2001) prove this point. The Independent on 8th May 2003 mentioned that 'while the majority of people (77%) describes themselves as Christians, it is also an elderly congregation compared with other religions. The proportion of people calling themselves Christians is lowest in the 16 to 24 age group, at less than 60%. But the same age band boasted the highest proportion of Muslims, 5%. There are of course people who do not see any merit in the idea of religious pluralism; they see religious diversity as a threat to their beliefs and claim exclusive validity for their beliefs and practices--'you are either with us or against us'. Then, there are others who are so indoctrinated with secular values that they consider religion itself as an anachronism. Although increased secularisation had paved the way for the decline of religion in the past, Britain's religious pluralism is giving rise to a sense of religious affiliation in many people. A quarter of people may identify themselves as atheists or agnostics, but public response to religion has become more ambivalent. People now feel more at home with different religious traditions, which are living side by side in peace and tolerance.

Religion in the Public Domain

In Britain the church was separated from the state long ago, but religion played a singular role in the British society in rituals and ceremonies, from state functions to family affairs. Although the House of Parliament is the symbol of secularism, the Sovereign remains the defender of the Faith, meaning Christianity, and Bishops have constitutional role in the House of Lords. Prince Charles now prefers to be the Defender of Faiths, not just Christianity. Religious educations syllabuses in schools and the presence of many state-funded religious denominational schools maintain the presence of religions in society. What have brought religion back in the public arena are the emergence of many non-Christian faiths on the one hand and the formation of some high profile faith or interfaith organisations since the 1980s. The following major organisations, some international, have been playing important role in this development:[93]

- The Inter Faith Network for the UK - Established in 1987 the Network has played a significant role in fostering good relations

between religious communities locally and nationally by fostering relationships through dialogue and co-operation. It represents
nine major faith communities in Britain, e.g., Baha'i, Buddhist,
Christian, Hindu, Jain, Jewish, Muslim, Sikh and Zoroastrian. All
member bodies of the Network subscribe to its document 'Building
Good Relations with People of Different Faiths and Beliefs'.

•   The Inner Cities Religious Council (ICRC) – ICRC is a five-
faith (Christian, Hindu, Jewish, Muslim and Sikh) council with
a strong Black Christian presence. Chaired by a minister from the
Office of the Deputy Prime Minister (ODPM) it attempts to tackle
regeneration policy issues on which DTLR takes the lead.

•   The Calamus Foundation – The Foundation is dedicated to
building bridges of understanding between followers of the three
Abrahamic faiths, i.e., Christianity, Islam and Judaism. It seeks to
emphasise the common ethical, moral, and historical roots of these
faiths and promotes interfaith dialogue.

•   Council of Christians and Jews - Inaugurated in 1942, the
Council aims to combat all forms of discrimination, prejudice and
intolerance, especially anti-Semitism, and to educate Christians and
Jews to appreciate each other's distinctive beliefs.

•   The Maimonides Foundation – The Foundation promotes
contact and understanding between Jews and people of other faiths
in the UK and abroad through dialogue and exchange of culture.

•   Three Faiths Forum – Established in 1997 the Forum encourages friendship, goodwill, and understanding and shared common
interests among Christians, Muslims and Jews. It also promotes the
training of ministers of religion to encourage respect for each other
on the basis of equality.

•   World Conference on Religion and Peace – Established in
1970 this multi-faith international organisation is dedicated to promoting cooperation among the world's religious communities with
an emphasis on putting in service the resources of each religious tradition for international peace

•   World Congress of Faiths – Established in 1936 it aims to create
understanding and a sense of unity and friendship between members
of the world's faiths through conferences, tours and other means.

Census 2001: Religion Matters in Britain

The UK is not only multi-racial and multi-ethnic but also a multi-faith society in which everyone has the right to practice religion. Religious organisations, centres and groups are free to conduct their affairs, promote their beliefs within the limits of the law, own property and run schools and a range of other charitable activities without any hindrance. Although Christianity remains the main religion, most of the world's religions are found to be practised in Britain. In addition to Hindu, Jewish, Muslim and Sikh communities there are smaller communities of Bahai, Buddhists, Jains and Zoroastrians. Then there are the followers of new religious movements. At the same time, there are many people who do not practise any religion and some reject religions outright. Organisations such as the British Humanist Associations and the National Secular Society represent some of these views.

The table below gives the 2001 UK population by religion.94 It has to be remembered that the question on religious identity was new in 2001 and was voluntary. In spite of this, 92.3% people chose to answer it. The total UK population was 58.8 million.

Religion	England	Scotland	Wales	N. Ireland	UK Total	UK %
Buddhist	139,046	6,380	5,407	533	151,816	0.3
Christian	35,251,244	3,294,595	2,087,242	1,446,386	42,079,417	71.6
Hindu	546,982	5,564	5,439	825	558,810	1.0
Jewish	257,671	6,448	2,256	365	266,740	0.5
Muslim	1,524,887	42,557	21,379	1,943	1,591,126	2.7
Sikh	327,343	6,572	2,015	219	336,149	0.6
Other	143,811	26,074	6,909	1,143	178,837	0.3
Total: All religions	38,190,984	3,389,490	2,131,007	1,451,414	45,162,895	76.8
No religion	7,171,332	1,394,460	537,935	NA	9,103,727	15.5

Not stated	3,776,515	278,061	234,143	NA	4,288,719	7.3
All: no religion / not stated	10,947,847	1,672,521	772,078	233,853	13,626,299	23.2

The inclusion of a religion question in the 2001 Census was a landmark event in British social and political history. It came only as a result of sustained and persistent campaign by the faith groups that began in the mid 1990s. The emergence of religious identity in modern Britain now gives British people the opportunity to legally express their chosen identity of faith or religion, in addition to their immutable identity of race or ethnicity. A number of institutions, some of them interfaith organisations, played a key role in seeing this through.[95] They are:

- The Inner Cities Religious Council (ICRC)
- The Interfaith Network
- Churches Working Together
- UK Action Committee on Islamic Affairs (later on, The Muslim Council of Britain)
- Office for National Statistics or ONS (later on, its Religious Affiliation Sub-Group)

The ICRC of the then Department of the Environment set the ball of religious question in the Census 2001 rolling in its meeting in January 1996. The Churches Working Together produced an influential paper linking the religious affiliation with matters of public policy in March of the same year. When the idea was put forward to the ONS, they understandably showed little enthusiasm in the idea. However, the alliance of faith groups was working hard to convince the ONS about the usefulness of this idea in the context of a new British society. As a result, the ONS formed a Religious Affiliation Sub-Group to work on a test question.

The Sub-Group, led by Professor Leslie Francis, initially discussed three aspects of religion, e.g., belief, practice and affiliation, deciding not to include the belief and practice aspects as they were considered as intrusions. They accepted to include only religious affiliation that relates to public and social dimensions of religion. Responses from various government departments ranged from enthusiasm to scepticism. Some were ambivalent. The ONS carried out a number of tests in 1997 that brought very positive outcomes.

The emergence of the Muslim Council of Britain in November 1997 brought a qualitative change in the campaign for the inclusion of religion in the 2001 Census. In a reception organised by the MCB on 2nd December 1998 the then Home Secretary Jack Straw supported the Muslim community's position on the census issue. In March 1999 the government published a white paper, The 2001 Census of Population, in which it recommended the religion question if there was sufficient public support. The MCB was trying strenuously to convince influential figures from all the political parties and conducted a census awareness campaign encouraging Muslim participation through all possible means, including publishing posters and writing articles.[96] The success of the campaign proved that if faith groups sincerely work together for a common purpose there is a greater likelihood of success. The simple question asked in the census was: "What is your religion?" The optional responses were:

- None
- Christian (including Church of England, Catholic, Protestant and all other Christian denominations)
- Buddhist
- Hindu

- Jewish
- Muslim
- Sikh
- Any other religion

The Challenge of Religious Discrimination

Discrimination is complex and involves not only race, gender and colour but also beliefs in cultural and religious difference. The famous Race Relations Act (1976) included the terms 'race, colour, nationality (including citizenship), ethnic or national origin'. During the process of formulating and enacting legislation the issue of religious markers of identity was not powerfully felt. In a quarter of a century, due to changing social circumstances, the feelings surrounding religious identity became more prominent. Thus, the issue of religious discrimination has come into prominence and Muslims are at the forefront of raising this issue.

Muslims, like other faith communities, enjoy the right to practice their religion, establish their religious centres and form organisations in Britain. They can also derive tax benefits for their places of worship and their marriage ceremonies are recognised. In lot of other areas in life, such as halal meat, their religious sensitivities are acknowledged.

However, it is also accepted that Muslims perceive and experience both religious and racial discrimination. The present anti-discrimination legislation, developed in piecemeal fashion, is insufficient in protecting Muslims and providing equal opportunities to them.[97] Jews and Sikhs are, however, protected because of their race. Thus tackling the issue of religious discrimination is important to Muslims. This has been triggered by Islamophobic attacks on Muslims and the lack of any legal recourse for this. Muslims are concerned that the race relations industry and the liberal intellectual camp are not sensitive enough to the pains Muslims suffer because of their religion.

Over the last few decades discrimination law in Britain addressed every major area of discrimination except religion. For Muslims and many other faith communities this is not fair, as religion is of prime importance in their lives. They often experience discrimination, prejudice and stereotypes that focus on their religious identity. With limited legal protection (i.e. only on the basis of race) they are vulnerable.

In a Home Office study of religious discrimination, two thirds of Muslim organisations reported unfair treatment resulting from school policies and practices and institutions of higher education. Three quarters reported unfair treatment from social service staff and from practices in social service departments. Compared with other faith groups Muslims reported the highest level of unfair treatment in employment".[98]

As the global awareness of religious identity is on the rise, many people in the world now feel proud to consider themselves as part of a religious community. This preference in their expression was encapsulated in a statement to the World Conference against Racism in South Africa in September 2001 by the Canadian representative who mentioned, 'there is a close, sometimes inseparable, relationship between discrimination based on religion and language and that which is based on racism and xenophobia'.[99]

Europe has also felt the necessity to redress its historical imbalance of keeping religion undervalued. The European Union's Article 13 of the Amsterdam Treaty (1999) included religious discrimination as a form of discrimination that all member states are expected to eliminate. As a result, the UK government has decided to outlaw religious discrimination in December 2003. The Crime and Disorder Act (1998), amended as a consequence of the Anti-Terrorism, Crime and Security Act (2001), now refers to offences that are 'racially or religiously aggravated'. This high profile reference to religion sets an important legal precedent in Britain. But such referenced are not a substitute for anti-discrimination laws vis-à-vis religion.

Opposition to outlaw religious discrimination in Britain is stronger in the secular liberal camp. The Rushdie affair in the late 1980s became the test case between freedom of expression and vilification of a religion. In their over-enthusiasm to support the author the left was were complaining against multiculturalism which they thought was fragmenting society. One ramification of the debate surrounding the saga was that religious groups, like race or gender groups, have a right not to be undermined or insulted in a pluralist society. 'In this particular instance their (Muslim) campaign did not succeed, but it has fired an important warning over the bows of those who believe that free society can allow anyone to say anything'.[100] There is a growing feeling that, as in education and politics, media and entertainment should also show sensitivity to people's religious sentiment.

Why is there a pressing demand to outlaw religious discrimination now? The answer is both religious and social. Many people want religious discrimination outlawed because at this period of history, where all other discriminations have been gradually outlawed, religion should also be included in this list. This coheres with contemporary ideas of equality, multiculturalism and social inclusion. Secondly, religion commands allegiance from a large section of Britain's population and they deserve respect from the law. Thirdly, a significant number of people, including many Muslims, put religion in the forefront of their personal and social life, not necessarily because they are fanatic or 'Islamist' per se, but because they are serious about what they believe and practise.

Religious discrimination is putting them in serious disadvantage as citizens of the country. The demand for outlawing religious discrimination and formation of a statutory religious equalities commission with a policing and monitoring brief is thus a legitimate one.

8. ISLAM AND BRITAIN'S MUSLIM COMMUNITY

Islam: A Brief Introduction

Human beings originated from a single soul.[101] Ever since the first man and woman stepped on the soil of earth with a divine task from God, their job, as His vicegerents, emissaries or representatives102 started with a monumental challenge. Unlike some religious beliefs that the first man and woman were sent down to earth as a punishment for the betrayal of their trust with God and wicked nature of woman, Islam is emphatic in telling that the first man and woman were only subjected to a test in heaven for a purpose. Both man and woman were equally responsible for their weaknesses. The Qur'anic verse 2:30 clarifies that human beings were originally destined to live on earth. However, before their arrival God put them on a test to prove that without His guidance human beings cannot perform their job as God's emissary. In that first test both man and woman proved susceptible to natural weakness. However, through their God-given knowledge and humility they immediately realised their mistake and sought forgiveness from their Lord. God, by His mercy, taught them how to repent and they were cleansed of their sins before coming to earth.[103]

The first man Adam was blessed with the capacity to learn and acquire knowledge. Adam's ability to name 'things' proved his competence in conceiving ideas and communicating this knowledge to others. The other creatures could not match his knowledge. The scepticism displayed by angels toward the creation of human beings was due to their lack of understanding of the divine purpose. Deeper knowledge gave the first man and woman the understanding and humility to seek repentance, whereas the arrogance of shallow knowledge brought downfall for Iblis who then became the Devil. Iblis was from among the Jinn, a creature with free will created before Adam. When angels realised that Adam was superior to them in certain knowledge they 'bowed down to Adam'.[104] Of course, human beings do not own knowledge, they were only bestowed with some by their Lord.

All human beings are born in nature (*fitra*), i.e., in the nature of self-surrendering to their Creator. 105 However, unlike angels, they are not 'programmed' to just obey God's command. In order to make human beings His wilful representatives on earth they were given the freedom to choose between good and evil.[106] This freedom to pick and choose has made human beings and Jinn folk unique in creation. The first man and woman chose to disobey God, but then they also chose to repent for their wrongdoing. Thus, along with the superiority in knowledge, the freedom to follow God has given human beings the edge over other creatures. Adam remained a wilfully obedient servant of God, a 'Muslim'. The words 'Islam' and 'Muslim' originate from the same Arabic root which means 'peace' and 'self-surrender'. It is in human nature to love peace through the self-surrender to God. According to a tradition of Prophet Muhammad, 'Every child is born in a state of nature (*Fitra*)...'[107]

According to Islam, it is forbidden to force people to adopt a certain religion or creed.[108] Islam, in its essence, calls for liberation of people intellectually. It not only allows but also promotes freedom of speech and the freedom to criticise in the society. The second Caliph of Islam, Umar ibn Al-Khattab once said, 'How dare you enslave people, when they were born free'?

As human beings' natural inclination is to submit to their Lord and they are sent to earth with the highest status,[109] they need to maintain this status through acquiring and developing their knowledge, improving their understanding and translating this knowledge into action. They are expected to study nature and reflect on the signs of creation around them, the natural and biological world. Islam encourages man to be aware that everything between the heaven and the earth follow guiding principles, *Sunan* in Arabic, in order to obey God. Everything is in full harmony and there is no discrepancy in creation. By obeying God human beings fit in the unique harmony with nature and come closer to Him.

God has assigned human beings to administer the earth by 'making subservient to them all that is in the heavens and all that is on earth'.[110] It is a demanding task and a serious test for human beings, as they have to maintain justice and balance in the creation. Individuals are to be judged in the hereafter for what they have done on earth. However, God has not left human beings bewildered and unguided. God foresaw that men and women would tend to forget their task and the 'worldly' preoccupation would drive their passion to do unworthy things. Family, social pressures and environment would lead them away from the straight path.

Also, as declared in the Qur'an, the Devil is lying in wait at every corner to jeopardise their journey to God[111] in order to take revenge for his own downfall.

In this challenging situation God has helped human beings in two ways. Firstly, He has not given the Devil any power to misguide people; he can only inspire and tempt. Secondly, God has sent certain righteous people, known as Prophets, to people to remind them of their task and warn them of the consequences if they misuse their trust with God.[112] The first man, Adam, was himself a Prophet who taught his progeny how to live as true servants of God. From Adam to Muhammad, all the Prophets were given exactly the same message, the message of teaching and leading humanity to the right path. All Prophets were 'Muslims'.

God created human beings out of love and made them into 'a single community'.[113] Their origin from a single pair and their transformation into communities and tribes are the manifestations of His creative wisdom in the diversity of human beings in terms of gender, race, colour and language.[114] As such, human beings are one community, one race. In His divine wisdom, God blessed them with different physical features, skin colours and languages so that they become signs for those who want to know.[115] Like the richness of colourful flowers in a garden human beings, as 'brothers (and sisters) to one another',[116] make the world inexorably meaningful.

Human beings' quest for knowing more, their creative innovation and adventurous mind has taken them to the four corners of the globe. Massive lands, islands, mountains and forests have succumbed to their explorative mind and resilient action. Although, as a result, they divided themselves into races and expressed themselves in different languages, they worked for their common destiny to make the world habitable and safe. They fought battles and wars and are still fighting, but their collective aspiration of making this earth peaceful and prosperous remains alive. With globalisation in most affairs of life this is now a big challenge for humanity.

The source being one, all people are the same. The same blood flows through everybody's veins. Although educational opportunities and other environment factors might create barriers between people which are artificial, no human being is superior over others except in God-consciousness, or *taqwa*.[117] Racism or racial hatred is thus the antithesis to human dignity. The reigning cruelty of present day capitalism and the fat arrogance of a few corporate giants might have divided the world, but one thing is becoming clearer that there cannot be any success for a minority at the cost of the majority. If only a tiny section of humanity thrives and the rest remains perpetually backward this defeats the purpose of human beings becoming a single community.

Islam is not an exclusive, sectarian, tribal or nationalistic religion. Tribes and races are for the adornment of human race. Racism is thus the antithesis to Islam. Muslims have generally upheld racial equality in history. Five times a day, weekly prayer congregations in each locality and the annual Hajj congregation in Makkah for Muslims from around the globe is testimony to the racial harmony of Islam. These and other compulsory rituals train Muslims daily, weekly and annually how to blend in their brotherhood for a common goal of making this world a better and just place. It is unfortunate that Muslims in the last few centuries lost many of their important values at their own peril. Truly, many Muslims are failing their Islam.

The following story tells how strongly the Prophet of Islam rejected racist feeling and racism.

A man once visited the Prophet's mosque in Madinah. There

he saw a group of people sitting and discussing their faith together. Among them were Salman who came from Persia, Suhaib who grew up in the Eastern Roman empire and was regarded as a Greek, and Bilal who was an African. The man then said: If the (Madinan) tribes of Aws and Khazraj support Muhammad, they are his people (i.e., Arabs like him). But what are these people doing here? The Prophet became very angry when this was reported to him. Straightway, he went to the mosque and summoned people to assemble. He then addressed them saying: 'O people, know that the Lord and Sustainer is One. Your ancestor is one, your faith is one. The Arabism of anyone of you is not from your mother or father. It is no more than a tongue (language).

It shows how he trained his people vis a vis human dignity and equality. The following traditions also clarify Islam's position on the uniqueness of the Muslim community on the one hand and human equality on the other:

> Oh people, remember that your Lord is One. An Arab has no superiority over a non-Arab nor a non-Arab has any superiority over an Arab; also a black man has no superiority over white man nor does a white man have any superiority over a black man, except by piety and good action. Indeed the best among you is the one with the best character. Listen to me, 'Did I convey this to you properly?" People responded, 'Yes, O Messenger of Allah.' The Prophet then said, each one of you who is here must convey this to everyone not present. (Excerpt from the Prophet's last sermon).

Indeed my friends and allies are not the tribe of so and so. Rather my friends and allies are the pious wherever they may be.[118]

Let people stop boasting about their ancestors. One is only a pious believer or miserable sinner. All men are sons of Adam, and Adam is made from dust.[119]

Madinah represented a perfect example of a pluralist society with people from different ethnicity, culture and religion.

Everyone became an indispensable part of the 'United Colours of Islam'. Muslim history subsequently saw the similar spirit of racial equality. In the heyday of the Muslim era, people were given value for their worth, not for their birth. People like Imam Bukhari from a predominantly Persian city became famous for collection of Hadith entitled Sahih al-Bukhari which has been unanimously declared by the scholars of Islam to be the most authentic book after the Qur'an. Throughout Muslim history Muslims of both Arab and non-Arab origin contributed to the human civilisation with same vigour. Professor A J Toynbee, in his *Civilisation on Trial* (New York, 1948) mentioned that, 'The extinction of race consciousness as between Muslims is one of the outstanding achievements of Islam, and in the contemporary world there is, as it happens, a crying need for the propagation of this Islamic virtue'. In the same way, H A R Gibb, in his Whither Islam (London, 1930) mentioned, 'No other society has such a record of success in uniting in an equality of status, of opportunity and endeavour so many and so varied races of mankind. The great Muslim communities of Africa, India and Indonesia, perhaps also the small community in Japan, show that Islam has still the power to reconcile apparently irreconcilable elements of race and tradition'.

In modern time Malcolm X of America and many other spirited celebrities talked about equality and brotherhood of Islam. Many have echoed Malcolm X's eulogy on the Muslim pilgrimage in Makkah and the spirit of brotherhood among people of diverse colours and races. In spite of many internal and external challenges Muslim societies have displayed resilience in maintaining racial tolerance. There may have been aspects of intolerance on the basis of politics and power in some parts of the Muslim world, but racism has always been the least important factor in the Muslim lands.

Muslims as a Community

Within the singularity of the human race God has blessed those who wilfully chose to live by the way of the Prophets. Prophets were the chosen leaders of humanity who formed one community, *ummah*. All of them submitted to the will of God. Establishing a community on the basis of belief, not race, tribe or language was unique in seventh century Arabia where the arrogance of racial or tribal superiority was at its peak. The tribal Arabs lived and died for their perceived racial superiority. This was termed 'a pit of fire'[120] from which God saved them. Islam, however, did not abolish tribal and other loyalties altogether. Contrary to the notion that those who embraced Islam had to forget their tribal and clan-affiliation, even the constitution of Madinah recognised individual tribes, albeit within the single Muslim *ummah*.

Muslims are one *ummah*.[121] The concept of one *ummah* has been so strong amongst Muslims that even in their period of decline and present day disunity they feel passionate about this. So, what is *ummah*? The word, extensively used in the Qur'an (sixty-four times), originates from the Arabic term '*umm*' meaning 'source, mother' and has many meanings. But the general meaning of the term is 'community'. Muhammad Asad, the famous western exegete of the Qur'an puts it as 'a group of living beings having certain characteristics or circumstances in common.'[122] *Ummah* is thus a broader community of people bonded by their desire to surrender to the will of God. The term *ummah* provides Muslims with a physical entity, bonded with brotherhood, through their fundamental beliefs of *Tawhid* (oneness of God), *Risalah* (prophethood) and *Akhirah* (life after death).

This idea of strong community feeling has come from the Qur'anic pronouncement that Muslims, the genuine believers, were made a 'justly balanced nation' or a 'middle nation'[123] and the 'best community'.[124] However, these attributes are condition-al. A community that professes Islam has to earn it by belief and action. Unlike the secular concept where nation state is the source of unity, faith defines the Muslim community which then subdivides into race, ethnicity or even present day nation states.

In the early period of Islam, Prophet Muhammad estab-lished a broader community, under the Charter or Constitution of Madinah, consisting of Muslims, Jews and even pagans who sided with the Prophet for freedom and justice. However, within that broader community there was the Muslim community consisting of Muslims from Makkah and the two tribes of Madinah. These first Muslims formed their well-knit community, as part of their self-definition. The relationship between Muslims was based on the twin concept of brotherhood and equality. The Muslim com-munity, under the authorised leadership of the Prophet and, later, the on Caliphs, identified themselves as one body. The Prophet's four rightly guided successors firmly established the foundation of a global community consisting of people from diverse backgrounds, but having the same values and vision of life. The legal, philo-sophical and intellectual basis of the *ummah* with its pluralist nature was thus firmly rooted.

Muslims belong to a global family and they are command-ed to remain united in the pursuit of Islam,[125] as 'all believ-ers are brethren'.[126] According to the traditions from Prophet Muhammad, 'You see the believers ... as if they were a single body; when one of its members is ailing, the rest of the body joins it in sleeplessness and fever'.[127] Also, 'The one who is not inter-ested in the affairs of Muslims is not one of them'.[128]

The Muslim passion for unity is thus important. After the demise of the rightly guided institution of the Caliphate Muslims were desperate to maintain this unity as an *ummah*, in terms of their global identity as Muslims and shared goodness among others in humanity. In the heydays of their political and intellectual power many Muslims travelled around the lands of Islam with the same rights and were generally embraced by other Muslims with unprecedented hospitality wherever they went. A Muslim from Tunisia could easily find a high-ranking government post in another Muslim land, say India, and vice versa. The global Muslim society was based on meritocracy.

Muslim governments and common people alike guarded this concept and feeling of oneness amongst Muslims. Although, since the beginning of eighteenth century they were losing their global position, the Muslim *ummah* remained one, at least symbolically, until the collapse of the Ottoman Caliphate in 1924. The spirit of oneness was so strong that after the Sepoy (soldiers) Mutiny against British rule in India in 1857, the British government had to obtain a sanction from the Ottoman caliph who advised Indian Muslims to remain loyal to Britain.[129]

The Muslim Legacy in Europe

When human sufferings in pre-Islamic *Jahiliyah* (ignorance) fourteen hundred years ago became unbearable, ordinary people were subjected to cruelty and racism by the ruling elite of the then powerful nations, Islam emerged with a message of hope for all. Arabia was then in the periphery of the 'civilised' world and known for its barbarism and extreme tribalism. Islam had only two messages that delivered this hope: firstly, the need for human beings' wilful submission to the one - and only - God, and secondly, the establishment of justice and equality in the society irrespective of gender, race or colour.

A people with a deeper consciousness of God and a true sense of responsibility emerged within a generation. This was history's biggest miracle. Islam came as a universal religion with a comprehensive way of life. It has never been a monolithic religion for a certain group of people. Muslims have always been multi-racial and multi-lingual themselves and at the same time they mostly lived in peace and harmony with others. Islam's inclusive nature tried to create rainbow societies wherever it went. Coexistence with other communities remained the hallmark of Islamic civilisation since its inception. Europe saw this in Spain and subsequently in most parts of the Ottoman Empire where Muslims, Christians and Jews lived in harmony and peace. When Muslims failed in their Islam they paid the penalty.

Conversely, what Europe experienced during this period was unfortunate religious intolerance, even within Christian churches, leading to many atrocities. Dogmatism, which was virtually unknown in Islam then, gave rise to forcible recanting and inquisitions in Europe during the Middle Ages. It is not surprising the first reports of ethnic cleansing in modern history happened with the removal of Muslims and Jews from Catholic Spain. Later on, the perpetuation of slavery and colonisation by European nations blighted their history, which is still haunting their conscience.

As long as Muslims collectively 'enjoined the right, forbade the wrong and believed in God' they had moral authority over others. But, as they became complacent with their past glory and their attachment to Islam grew thinner they were going down the slippery slope of stagnation in almost all spheres of life. When Europe reinvented its potential through the Renaissance the Muslim world was losing power and dignity. The continuous political, military and intellectual peril of the Muslim world became acute during the last few centuries and almost the entire Muslim world came under European hegemony by the end of ninteenth century.

During this colonial period the Muslim *ummah* underwent a catalogue of disasters. The vanguard of Muslim socio-economic and political structure, the *Shariah,* on the one hand and religious *Awqaf* (charitable endowment) on the other, were gradually forced out or phased out from the Muslim lands. Intellectual stagnation set in and Muslim societies lost their dynamism. From Morocco to Indonesia the situation was similar. Towards the end of this downturn, the once powerful Ottoman Empire came to be known as the 'sick man of Europe'. The pandemonium continued decade after decade and in 1924 the weak Ottoman power collapsed. Muslim glory formally vanished. This has had a far-reaching effect on the Muslim psyche ever since.

The post-1924 Muslim world has been chaotic and pessimistic. However, concerned Muslims across the world never gave up their campaign of reviving the *ummah* from within. Various Muslim individuals and groups emerged to fight for the independence of their lands, gradually taking the shape of freedom movements in different parts of the Muslim world. During the Second World War Muslim leaders in different parts of the world were mapping out their strategies for political independence. By the end of the war the European powers could no longer cope with the rising tide of these freedom movements and most Muslim lands became independent by the middle of the century.

However, the outgoing European powers adopted some insidious ploys to maintain control over the future Muslim countries. Arbitrary division of lands, transplantation of hostile communities within the population and, above all, the imposition of secular and corrupt leaders on the people became the hallmark of European retreat from the Muslim world. The influence of narrow nationalism borrowed from Europe and intolerant sectarianism from within became tools of division and the tyrannical regimes took advantage of these to rule Muslim lands, thus keeping Muslims divided. The rebuilding of Muslim lands remains difficult.

Nationalism in its present form developed in Europe at the end of the nineteenth century and matured in the beginning of twentieth century. In the Middle Ages it had hardly any trace in any part of the world, for there were no nation states in those days.[130] The basis of popular loyalty was religion then, in Europe it was Christianity. The rise of nationalistic sentiment in Europe became the rallying point of warmongers to such an extent that questions were raised whether 'nationalism is taking the place of religion as the principle of governing all social and intellectual life'.[131] The two catastrophic World Wars that changed the world were rooted in extreme nationalism. Nationalism became a powerful weapon to divide the Turks and the Arabs, ultimately destroying the weakened Ottoman Caliphate. The Republican Turkish leadership was so intoxicated by nationalistic fervour that they made attempts to oust everything related to Arabs, including Islam and the Arabic language from Turkey. The Turkish people became illiterate overnight when Arabic was banned. No wonder the orientalist Bernard Lewis considers nationalism as man's newfound idol.

Another such struggle is being fought in our own time - not against Al-Lat and Al-Uzza (pre-Islamic objects of worship) - but a new set of idols called states, races and nations: this time it is the idols that seem to be victorious.[132]

The post-independent Muslim world remained weak due to the social, political and economic mismanagement, ineptitude and corruption of its leaders and general passivity of the Muslim population. What we see today is the legacy of the past few decades. Much of Muslim world today is poor and all of it is technologically backward and politically weak. In most countries they are ruled by armed ruling minorities who are at loggerheads with their own people. The remnant of colonial education system is compounding the problem; producing generations of strangers within Islam. Colonialism had a deepening impact on them – physically, politically, economically, culturally and intellectually. As a result, in spite of huge population and tremendous natural resources, Muslims are now the underdogs in most places, and victims of atrocities in some parts of the world. Today, according to the UNHCR, more than four-fifth of the world's refugees are Muslims. The trauma of war, political violence and economic poverty are taking their toll on Muslim psyche. The growing Muslim settlement in the West is partly a legacy of this painful situation.

Since the 1990s the situation has taken a new shape. The genocide of Balkan Muslims, the wholesale destruction of Chechnya, the continuous occupation of Palestine and Kashmir are not only considered as unjust to Muslims but also treated as scars to humanity. The forced regime change in Afghanistan and Iraq has added salt to the wounds. Additionally, a section of the western media depicts Islam as a rigid and obscurant religion and Muslims as fanatical, terror-prone people; feeding people with prejudices and thereby encouraging discrimination against and the marginalisation of Muslims in many western countries. The sad fact is that until recently there is was no precedent for religious coexistence in Europe. The historic belief by the church that there is 'no salvation outside the church' made this intolerance a religious one. This has contributed to the xenophobic feeling amongst some Europeans regarding Muslims. Although, since the Second Vatican Council Islam has been given some status, Prophet Muhammad is still shunned as a guide and Qur'an is not treated as God's word.

Against this backdrop it is not difficult to understand why Muslims find it hard to be genuinely accepted as equal citizens in European countries. However, post war Europe including Britain has come a long way from this intolerance, albeit from a racial point of view. Racial intolerance has definitely reduced in Britain. What about religious intolerance? This is the area where many well-meaning people are working hard. One may argue that like the rest of Europe, Britain has also become an irreligious country where religion is cornered to an individual and private set of beliefs, so there is no relevance of religion in modern Europe. But, this is not true. With the recent emergence of faith agenda in the public arena religion is now reclaiming its lost territories. The adoption of the human rights bills and conventions helped religion make its mark in the public domain. Acceptance of religious pluralism does now seem to be a major point of discussion in various circles. This has been addressed elsewhere in the book.

Evolution of the Muslim Community in Britain

The history of Muslim interaction with Britain is a long and deep-rooted one. It included people of all spectra, including those in the higher echelon of the society. The relationship between the United Kingdom and the Muslim world dates back hundreds of years, with contact in some shape or form almost since the advent of Islam in the seventh century.[133]

The first and most prominent personality linked with this relationship was the Anglo-Saxon King Offa (died 796 CE), who had coins minted with the Islamic declaration of faith in Arabic, 'there is no God except Allah, Muhammad is His Messenger'.[134] Since then Britain took interest in improving its relationship with the Muslim world through academic and diplomatic means. The translation of Arabic books, the most important of them was Al-Khawarazimi's '*Kitab al Jabr w'al-Muqabbal*' rendered by Robert Chester into Latin in 1145,[135] was an important step in this process. Arabic became a lingua-franca for European scholars and Muslim intellectual giants like Razi, Ibn Sina, Ibn Rushd became familiar names in academic circles. Ibn Sina's 'Cannon of Medicine' was a standard text for medical students in Europe well into the seventeenth century. Muslims also revived the knowledge of the Greek and Indian philosophers in their heydays of intellectual discourse, which in turn benefited Europe.

The military encounters during the European Crusades against the Muslims and the enlightening Muslim civilisation in Spain also became the gateway of Muslim knowledge into Britain. During sixteenth and seventeenth centuries when the Muslim power was waning in the East, Muslim naval power dominated the Mediterranean. 'When the threat of Spanish Armada loomed in the mid 1580's, Queen Elizabeth did not hesitate to ask the Ottoman Sultan Murad for naval assistance against the Spaniards'.[136] Islam continued to influence Britain's academic and religious life over the following centuries. 'Texts in Arabic in mathematics, astronomy, chemistry and medicine were central to higher education in England in the seventeenth century'.[137] In English intellectual circles knowing Arabic and discussing the works of prominent Muslim scientists was common.

However, the first sizable Muslim presence started during Britain's colonial period. Muslim seamen (known as 'lascars'), soldiers and students established the first communities in the ports of England and Scotland.[138] The nascent Muslim community achieved prominence with the conversion of William Henry Quillium of Liverpool, a solicitor who was given the title of 'Sheikh-ul-Islam of the British Isles' following his visit to Turkey, and the establishment of the Shah Jehan Mosque in Woking in 1889. The mosque still exists today.

By the turn of the century, Syed Ameer Ali, the first Indian Privy Councillor, established a 'London Muslim Fund' in 1910 for 'a mosque in London worthy of the tradition of Islam and worthy of the capital of the British Empire'.[139] That, later on, became instrumental in establishing the East London Mosque in 1941 in the London borough of Tower Hamlets which now has the highest number of Muslims in any inner city borough. Jamiat Muslimeen, a voluntary service organisation, was formed to run the mosque and community activities. The Jamiat still remains at the forefront of the management of this mosque. In 1944 King George VI visited the Islamic Cultural Centre (The Central Mosque) for its official opening.

During the first few decades of the twentieth century prominent Muslims of English origin, e.g., Lord Headley and Marmaduke Pickthal, became the vocal exponents of Islam in British public life. A number of Muslim scholars from British India, e.g., Syed Ameer Ali, Yusuf Ali and Hasan Suhrawardi, made their contribution to the evolution of the Muslim community during this period.

Post-war Britain saw an influx of Muslims from many commonwealth countries. However, the emphasis of Muslim activities shifted towards the establishment of social, educational and welfare institutions.[140] In the 1960s organisation like the Federation of Students Islamic Societies, UK Islamic Mission and the Muslim Educational Trust emerged. In the 1970s various organisations and centres arose to cater for the growing needs of the Muslim community, e.g., The Union of Muslim Organisations, Impact International, the Islamic Foundation, Islamic Council of Europe, etc.

The first generation Muslims in the emerging Muslim community, till 1970s, were in dilemma as to whether they would finally settle in Britain or go back to their countries of origin. However, as the younger generation were growing up in British environment the option was becoming less practical. During the 1980s and 1990s Muslims were embarking on a series of positive steps for the realisation of their educational, social and political rights. They were also learning how to effectively engage with others to pursue common good for all in mainstream society. The 1990s saw a new wave of Islamophobia due to some unforeseen factors, e.g., the Rushdie affair, the Gulf War and the genocide of Balkan Muslims in the heart of Europe. Muslims further realised that their progress as a faith community was linked with other faith communities. The formation of a Muslim umbrella group, the Muslim Council of Britain (MCB) in 1997, and the publication of the Runnymede Trust's report on Islamophobia in the same year helped Muslims to assert their presence.

However, the world suddenly became a difficult place for Muslims of Britain after two events in 2001 and threw the community into crisis management mode. The first was the summer disturbances involving Muslim youth, for the first time, in three cities of northern England and the second was the devastating terrorist attack on America by terrorists of alleged Muslim link. The wars and the subsequent occupation of Afghanistan and Iraq by America have put further challenges before the Muslim community everywhere including Britain. Britain's involvement in the Iraq War has soured the relationship between the British Muslim community and the New Labour government. However, as most British people were against the war this has opened the door of opportunity for Muslims to work closely with them. Muslims, particularly the youth, have now a monumental task to strengthen their community and make a positive contribution to the wider society.

Muslims are now a part and parcel of the British society. They are young, diverse and multi-racial. The Parekh Report, *The Future of Multi-Ethnic Britain*, published in 2000 by the Runnymede Trust, suggests that major communities like Muslims should not be seen as monolithic, separate, inferior, or as the enemy, manipulative or cynical. Now that religion has become a part of the census report, thanks to the campaign initiated by Muslims and other faith communities, all religious communities can raise their voice on the basis of information by the census. This is a tremendous achievement in the midst of a powerful secular trend in Britain.

The richness of the Muslim community today reflects the microcosmic nature of the *ummah*. Muslims are vibrant in many spheres of life. They are from the four corners of the world, including European and home-grown British Muslims. According to the 2001 Census, 11.6% of Muslims are white, 6.9% are black and 74% are Asian or Asian British.[141] For historical reasons various communities have concentrated in places of their choice, e.g., Pakistanis in Bradford, Bangladeshis in London's Tower Hamlets. They are also diverse in terms of their theological, cultural, political and linguistic varieties. Most trends in Muslim countries are replicated in Britain. There are varying Islamic traditions, e.g., Sufis, Tablighis, Salafis, Debandis and Barelwis on the one hand and traditional and modernists on the other. Together they make the mosaic of the *ummah* in Britain.

Some Muslims also have an impressive and growing social and economic infra-structure across the country. With higher than average birth-rate, labour migration, oversees students, war refugees and asylum seekers the number is growing. Including the

Balkans, Muslims number twenty million in Europe.

Numbering nearly 1.6 million (2.7% of total British population, 3.1% of the population of England), according to the 2001
Census, Muslims are the largest religious minority in the country.
The census has shown that most Muslims in Britain are British citizens. The numbers of British-born and indigenous Muslims now
outnumber the first generation immigrant people from different
continents.

Muslims are spread out across the British Isle, although they
are concentrated in important cities across the Midlands and
Yorkshire. London has the highest number of Muslims (607,083;
8.5% of its population) in the country. The London borough
of Tower Hamlets has the highest concentration of Muslims
(36.4%) followed by Newham (24.3%). Birmingham with 140,017
Muslims (14.3%) and Bradford with 75,201 Muslims (16.08%) are
the important city councils with high Muslim concentrations.[142]
A press release issued by the Office for National Statistics (ONS)
on 7 May 2003 mentioned that 'Britain's Muslim community has a
high proportion of young people – 33.8% of Muslims are aged 0-
15 (national average 20.2%) and 18.2% of age 16-24 (national average 10.9%).

The Challenges

Unfortunately, however, a section of the British media loves
to link Muslims with something that evokes fear and sarcasm,
e.g., fanatical bearded mullahs, extremists, rich oil sheikhs or
veiled women. Under such stereotypes Islam is portrayed as an
intolerant, militant and rigid religion and, as such, Muslims suffer from discrimination, hate and various forms of attack. This
'religious racism' against Muslims has increased considerably
post-September 11 and is exacerbating the 'clash of civilisation'

concept. This is putting pressure on the peaceful coexistence of communities in many western countries, including Britain. The divisive concept of 'us' and 'them' seems to be on the rise and could undermine community cohesion in society. Some Muslims fear that after the collapse of Communism, Islam is now seen as the 'villain' of the free world. The negative portrayal of the Muslim community would have negative effect not only on social and political life, but also on individuals.

The simplistic view of seeing Islam and Muslims in a linear way is borne out of ignorance and historical prejudice. People need only ask themselves two basic questions about this Abrahamic religion and its diverse people to achieve a balanced view of it: (1) How has Islam been able to bring together in a great religious family such diverse people of all races and maintain a dazzling civilisation for so long? (2) Why do a quarter of world's people across the globe confess Islam, in spite of their fragmentation over a long period and present sufferings from internal despots and external aggression?

Britain's current anti-discrimination laws are inadequate to give Muslims and other non-Christian groups legal protection. The failure of existing race relations legislation to cover religion has contributed to the vulnerability of these communities. At the same time, occasional mixed messages from politicians and government ministers are putting Muslims particularly in further difficulties. In recent years the assimilationist tone in the government white paper on immigration, 'Secure Borders, Safe Havens' of 2002, the insensitive use of the term 'swamping' in relation to asylum seekers, most of whom are desperate Muslims fleeing from many parts of the world, and accusation hurled on Muslims as 'isolationist' does not help the community.

These factors, coupled with some of their own weaknesses,

have put the Muslim community in a challenging situation. It is true that many Muslims were at the bottom of the socio-economic ladder when they first came to Britain.[143] They inevitably experienced unemployment, poor working conditions, poverty, poor and over-crowded housing, poor health, and low educational qualifications.[144] Unfortunately, over the last few decades, things have not changed much. There is still multiple deprivation of the community in education, employment, housing, health, and political voice.

Although there are successful business ventures in property, food and small-scale enterprises on the one hand and there are many doctors, engineers and other professionals on the other in the Muslim community, they still have a very high unemployment rate in Britain. The Muslim community may boast of its many thousand millionaires, but Pakistani and Bangladeshi people are still the most deprived minority ethnic groups in Britain. They are more likely to be unemployed than other Asians, let alone compared to the white population.

Muslims generally live in clusters in inner cities across Britain. Pakistanis and Bangladeshis generally live in overcrowded council or housing association properties lacking in basic amenities. As a result, they are generally segregated from their fellow white citizens and the education of their children is hampered. In a recent survey of Muslim opinion most Muslim organisations questioned identified staff, policies and practices of landlords, local authorities, housing associations, estate agents as sources of unfair treatment.[145] Muslim concentrated areas have the highest deprivation ranking index in Britain.[146]

In education, particularly at the GCSE level, Muslim children have lower than average achievement rate. Although this has slightly improved over the last few years and Pakistani and

Bangladeshi children respectably had 40% and 45% good GCSE grades (5 A*-C) compared to the 51% national average in 2002, this has its effect in the employment market.[147]

In areas of health many first generation Muslims have irregular food habits, lack of exercise and difficulties related to crammed accommodation. Muslims generally have a high number of chronic illnesses, including heart disease. Recently the medical professionals have reported a rise in Muslim mental health patients. There are insufficient faith related provisions for Muslim patients.

In politics Muslims have the poorest representations in both the Houses of Parliament and European Parliament. Although there are now a good number of Muslim councillors in some inner cities from among the three main political parties their social influence, locally and nationally, is insignificant.[148] The lack of Muslim presence in the upper echelons of the civil service, media, criminal justice system and other important areas is undermining their rightful place in society.

Multiple deprivation factors, combined with their alienating effects on Muslim youth, have the potential of creating further image problem for Muslims and thus creating more difficulties in their social integration. Many people in the establishment blame Muslims and Asians for isolationism without accepting the fact that positive integration is a two way process. Muslims see the lack of reciprocity to genuinely engage them in public domain from some powerful quarters in the country.

The worry in the community about drugs, drug related offences and youth criminality is increasing. There are now a disproportionate numbers of Muslims, mainly among the youth, in British prisons (which is 8.5% of the prison population, compared to their 2.7% national average). In 1991 there were only 731

Muslims in prisons.[149]

On the negative side there are signs that a sizeable body of Muslim youth is increasingly turning into a kind of underclass. They do badly in schools and face poor job prospects. They are alienated from both their parental and the wider British culture and nurture a strong sense of victimhood.[150]

As the Muslim community is evolving with its strengths and weaknesses in pluralist Britain there are broadly three trends among Muslims, particularly the youth.[151]

- A small number of vocal Muslim youth have become frustrated and angry thus radicalised due to various internal and external factors. They generally subscribe to and promote social ghettoisation for Muslims in non-Muslim environment. Their overt radicalism is often used by the opportunistic section in the establishment, especially the media, to create barriers between Muslims and wider society.

- A significant group have now become very 'casual' Muslims and some in this trend are even embarrassed to identify themselves openly as Muslims. They have undertaken, probably without proper understanding, an assimilationist approach in cultural aspects.

- A large group are maintaining their faith and Muslim identity with confidence. In their 'middle-path' approach they do not see their Muslimness as an obstacle to contributing and socially integrating with others. They are convinced that Islam can flourish positively in a genuinely pluralistic environment.

This is not unique to the Muslim community alone, other minority communities display similar features. It is encouraging that the number of Muslims subscribing to ghettoisation is on the wane. The main challenge for the Muslim community is the gradual dilution of Islamic attachment because of the overwhelming secular materialistic nature of British life.

In spite of multiple deprivation and negative media image the Muslim community is rich with good individuals, families and groups who have used their talents, skills and resources. Muslims are now generally becoming more assertive and gaining more confidence in all areas of life, from education to politics, and are now in a position to contribute in shaping modern Britain. The younger generation of Muslims are now becoming more pragmatic and realising that their future progress lies in their strength as a community and ability to engage proactively with others for the common good.

9. MUSLIM IDENTITY IN BRITAIN

Identity, Youth Culture and its Manifestations

What is meant by 'identity' and how does it affect an individual within a community or society? What influence does one's ethnicity, religion, language, nationality or other aspects of life have on his or her identity? Are different aspects of identity mutually exclusive? This also raises a bigger question as to the essence of the human identity in the post-modern era; should it be determined by the factors mentioned above or is identity merely a myth of ever changing reality as the proponents of post-Modernism want us to believe? These issues are not purely academic; they are relevant in one's day to day life.

Secondly, what does identity mean to Muslim individuals who claim themselves as being part of their wider community or ummah? How does it affect Muslim youth, especially in the West, when they are continually being targeted for proselytisation by the secular materialistic world-view and always reminded about it?

From a sociological point of view, identity is a sense of personhood that involves sameness as well as difference, i.e., it tells us what kind of person one is compared to another. It also tells of the uniqueness of human diversity in this world. As the individual and society are intertwined, questions arise as to whether individuals as 'creators of society', are more important or whether society with its tremendous influence dictates individuals. The first approach stresses that individuals as agents of changes and with free choice, make their decisions to construct society. This 'interactionist' approach empowers individuals to look into themselves for their inherent capabilities so that they play meaningful roles as movers and shakers of society. This tells us how human beings are ever creative and dynamic to overcome natural and environmental impediments. On the other hand, the second approach suggests that individuals are mere tools or products of society, because of the latter's over-riding influence on the former. Individuals may be creative and dynamic, but in this 'deterministic' approach they are constrained by events beyond their control in the society. As such, they conform to society in the end.

This is a big sociological as well as theological debate and some proponents in modern sociology have come with a middle-of-the-road approach which is nearer to the Islamic approach. This 'structuration' theory tends to harmonise the relationship between individuals and society by emphasising that they are complementary to each other, not competitive. Individuals have the capacity to create a society and society has also tremendous influence on individuals. The micro-individual and macro-social perspectives are not mutually exclusive, according to this idea.

There are multiple aspects of one's identity. Some aspects of it are immutable, e.g., race, ethnicity, colour, gender, age or physical feature. One is born with them and has no choice but to live with them, even if they do not feel comfortable with these aspects of their identity. As human beings have no control over these, decent people accept this human diversity as a natural phenomenon and keep away from arrogance on any aspect of this identity. Society accepts this diversity as its strength rather than its weakness. On the other hand, the aspects of identity that can be changed are faith, religion, language, cultural habits, citizenship and certain social statuses. Most of these are non-immutable, i.e., changeable. They are choice-based human features and individuals have the option of changing them. Many people change some aspects of their identity over their lifetime. Individuals and society are also expected to value and respect this choice-based identity upheld by people.

Some areas of identity impact on an individual's daily life. Jobs, place of living or neighbourhood, their support for a football or cricket club, etc, are important in their regular life. Not all aspects of this identity are manifested at all times. Depending on the socio-economic context, some of them may wield disproportionate influence on individuals and communities. It is the prevailing situation that determines which aspect gets more prominence.

Identity is heavily influenced by cultures and sub-cultures within a community or a group of people. In almost every society there are some distinctive sub-cultures. Some of them may be in direct opposition to the mainstream cultures and can clash. Examples include youth subculture, working class subculture and minority subculture (there may even be subcultures within a minority subculture). Depending on social harmony and stability they can be the gems and assets of a society. The whole society can and should feel proud of this diversity.

For a confident individual all these aspects of identity are complementary and thus encouraging. In a decent pluralist society they do not contradict with each other and individuals feel proud, not arrogant, of their own identity. A society with an open view of its diverse communities considers them as its strength, not its weakness. On the other hand, a society with a closed view sees them as its weakness and a danger to it. The following list from a report by The Runnymede Trust highlights two views on this.[152] The open views of others give individuals and communities the confidence to work in harmony with all. Tolerance, recognition and the celebration of people's diversity are not only important to people's immutable identities but also to their chosen identities. Choice and diversity represent the rainbow of a society, as people with diverse background are the mosaic of the human race.

Table 9.1 Closed and open views of the other

Distinctions	Closed views	Open views
Monolithic/Diverse	The Other seen as a single monolithic bloc, static and unresponsive to new realities.	The Other seen as diverse and progressive, with internal differences, debates and development.
Separate/Interacting	The Other seen as separate; (a) not having any aims or values in common with the self; (b) not affected by it; (c) not influencing it.	The Other seen as independent with the self: (a) having certain shared value and aims; (b) affected by it; (c) enriching it.
Inferior/Different	The Other seen as inferior to the self: e.g. barbaric, irrational, 'fundamentalist'.	The Other seen as different but of equal worth.
Enemy/Partner	The Other seen as violent, aggressive, threatening, to be defeated and perhaps dominated.	The Other seen as an actual or potential partner in joint co-operative enterprises and in the solution of shared problems.

Manipulative/Sincere	The Other seen as manipulative and deceitful, bent only on material or strategic advantage.	The Other seen as sincere in their beliefs, not hypocritical.
Criticisms of the self rejected/considered	Criticisms made by the Other of the self are rejected out of hand.	Criticisms of the self are considered and debated.
Discrimination defended/criticised	Hostility towards the Other used to justify discriminatory practises and exclusion of the Other from mainstream society.	Debates and disagreements with the Other do not diminish efforts to combat discrimination and exclusion.
Hostility towards the Other seen as natural/problematic	Fear and hostility towards the Other accepted as natural and 'normal'.	Critical views of the Other themselves subjected to critique, lest they be inaccurate and unfair.

Unfortunately, some communities in certain periods of history had faced difficulties in living with their different aspects of identity. This is a historical phenomenon of human deviation that gave rise to atrocities and, in worst cases, 'ethnic cleansing'. In recent history, the Jews in Nazi Germany, the Blacks in apartheid South Africa and the Palestinians in Israel have undergone horrible sufferings because of their race or religion. Today, Muslims in some countries are going through similar experiences of suffering because of their racial as well as religious identities.

The youth are the most dynamic and energetic section of any society. As the youth of today are destined to take over the affairs of the society of tomorrow, they always attract serious attention from all, starting from the political establishments to religious bodies. Societies need to ensure order, stability and continuity, and in this the youth have a unique role to play in carrying forward the values of society. When children learn skills and the values needed to become fully contributing members of their society through formal and informal education they go through various rites of passage. Developed societies take initiative in transmitting these rites of passage through various methods.

What we see as youth culture in the West today which is also influencing the rest of the world, developed after the Second World War. The factors, so far, that have shaped this culture are increased commercialisation and consumerism which was targeted to maximise profit from the youth market with products, such as designer clothes, music records and CDs; the influence of mass media, including radio, TV, magazines; increased participation in higher education; growing affluence of young people with cash and credit cards to spend on easily available consumer products; and rapid transition from the traditional, value-laden life to a permissive and laissez faire lifestyle.

The transition from childhood to adulthood, i.e., adolescence, is generally a difficult period when the search for identity is a determinant factor for young people. This is the period when young people want to explore the world in an adult way as they change physically, emotionally and socially. There is a gender variation in this process, as boys and girls develop differently. At the same time, the social and economic class of people as well as their ethnicity and religion have an impact on the development of youth and their attitude to life.

Individuals achieve a sense of identity depending on their up-bringing and environment. The manifestation of this identity becomes clear through various attributes, e.g., how they talk, behave and dress. Youth culture provides emotional security to the youth in this difficult period of transition from childhood to adulthood. Those who can successfully sail through this transition become more autonomous, attain a positive self-belief and develop good relationships with their parents and other adults in society. On the other hand, a weak sense of identity makes young people vulnerable and unsettled, which then influences negatively in their future life. Some of them may end up 'acting out' through delinquency and criminality. 'Territorial' gang fighting now prevalent in some inner city areas is a crude example of this 'acting out'. Others simply 'act in' and become dejected. Many youth, particularly from minority communities, may suffer from lack of self-esteem and apathy.

A positive family upbringing as well as an inclusive social and educational environment helps develop positive youth culture in a society that aids the smooth transition in their adolescence. This benefits every young person from the majority and minority communities. On the other hand, when a society is fragmented, communities fractured and families broken and education remains non-inclusive, many in the young generation grow up with a sense of disaffection. A tiny section of youth may prosper in this situation, but that does not help the society. No society can progress when its fabric is destroyed.

The diversity and uniqueness of human beings are a cause for celebration, not concern, in a pluralist society. Diversity is an asset, not a liability. The colourful rainbow of the human race declares the equal worth of everyone, irrespective of their status or background. Unfortunately, the manifestation of one's identity often creates strong feelings, if not hatred, in some people who do not see things broadly. This is a challenge for all in society. The following list of such manifestations is not an exhaustive one.

Table 9.2 Manifestations of Identity

Manifestation of identity	Examples
1. Faith/belief	The belief system, i.e., whether and how someone believes in monotheism, trinity, original sin, etc.
2. Marriage/Family	Issues regarding marriage, man–woman relationship, extended family structure and family ethos, etc.
3. Appearance/clothes	Cultural and religious expressions regarding modesty and beauty, likes and dislikes, e.g., dress for men and women, beards, hairstyle.
4. Food/eating habits	Type of food and drinks and how they are consumed, e.g., alcohol, pork, Halal or Kosher.
5. Social Life	Visits, family gatherings, pub culture, etc.
6. Rituals	Prayer and prayer facilities, holidays, pilgrimage, etc.
7. Creative expressions	Art, calligraphy, poem, music, dance, drama, architecture, e.g., minarets.
8. Celebration/entertainment	Religious, historical and national, e.g., Eid, Diwali, Hanuka, Christmas.
9. Verbal expressions	Vocabulary, terminology and expression.
10. Visits and holidays	Time and places people visit and go for holiday.
11. Inter-generational interaction	Respect and sensitivity while people of different generations talk and interact.
12. Economic habit	Income, expenditure, investment, issue of financial ethics, e.g., interest.
13. Illness and bereavement	Religious and cultural requirement as well as taboos surrounding them.

Factors that Affect Identity

Identity, in the broader sense, is derived from the attachment individuals have with their family, community and society. The historical lineage of the family and the evolution of the community as well as the contemporary challenges and opportunities within a social context play an important part in forming this identity. The inner feelings of individuals borne out of these factors are then broadly manifested in their external person. The factors that help to create a broader identity of an individual at the macro-level are as follows.

On the other hand, the micro-identity of individuals is heavily influenced by factors relevant to their day to day encounters in life. These real life experiences dictate their behaviour pattern which, over time, contributes to building their personality. People either want to identify themselves in certain manners or their identity is defined by the expectation of others. The media now probably play the most important part in this characterisation. All these aspects often create challenges in the society. The factors that contribute to one's micro-identity are as follows:

Assimilation versus Integration

Assimilation is primarily a cultural concept where minority communities merge with the majority dominant one in a cultural melting pot. The concept was used in American race relations after the Second World War to mean the gradual dissolving of immigrant groups into the dominant white American society, vaguely termed as 'American values'. However, assimilation could also mean the resultant product of dominant and minority cultures fusing together, although dominant culture would have an edge over the others. There is a fear in the minority communities about the term 'assimilation', as it tends to create often undesired homogeneity within communities. In Britain this approach was rejected by an influential Labour politician, Roy Jenkins, in 1966 who insisted on the 'cultural diversity, coupled with equal opportunity in an atmosphere of mutual tolerance'.[153] This set the tone of multiculturalism in Britain since then, which for so long intended to strengthen social or cultural pluralism.

On the other hand, 'integration' is primarily a social concept that looks for open interaction and engagement among communities in order to create a rainbow society. It is a process by which communities have closer social, cultural, economic and political relationships, without the threat of being merged into one another. Through interaction, accommodation, mutual acceptance and maybe healthy competition, members of minority communities can enjoy equality in respect of their civil rights and obligations but keep their independent community identity.

In an assimilationist approach communities lose out and individual identity gets weaker to the peril of all at the end. On the other hand, communities feel safe and confident in a genuinely integrationist approach and individuals gain much from it. When a society becomes a wider community of communities with tolerance and respect for others, people from all backgrounds feel enthusiasm in strengthening it. With confident individuals working for the betterment of the society everybody benefits. As minority communities always worry about being 'swallowed' by the dominant mainstream culture, particularly in the beginning stage of their settlement, the policy makers and influential people from the latter need to show sensitivity in their approach toward the former.

Identity and Citizenship

Citizenship is primarily a political concept that provides access to rights and powers on the one hand and duties and responsibilities on the other. Citizenship gives the legal right to belong to a country. The present idea of citizenship is now very much linked to the concept of nation states with geographical boundaries. Citizenship rights and responsibilities are intertwined. The rights of a citizen are generally as follows: a) civic rights, e.g., freedom of speech and equality before law; b) political rights, e.g., right to vote and to organise politically; and c) socio-economic rights, e.g., social security and economic welfare.

On the other hand, citizens are bound by contract, sometimes unwritten, with the nation state or country, i.e., its constitution and laws. The demand for an individual's allegiance to a country can sometimes clash with their conscience and religious morality. In such a case they have to make a good judgement and see whether the source of the demand is the government in power. In any case, a citizen is not bound to obey an unjust decision from a government, no matter what the threat or actual penalty may be. Human beings cannot compromise with justice and international legality.

Muslim scholars throughout history have articulated these rights of individuals and categorised them, in order of priority. In Islam, *Shariah* or Islamic law is designed to benefit the individual and the community at large. Establishing and maintaining justice (*adl* or *qist* in Arabic) is at the core of these benefits. The objective of Islamic Law is to benefit (*maslaha* in Arabic) people.[154] It is only to bring justice among human beings that God sent His Prophets and the Holy Books to this world.[155] These benefits or public interests have been classified into three descending categories of importance. They are:

> 1. *Dharuriyat* (essential) - without which religion and, in essence, human life becomes meaningless. The essential objectives are those divine rights of individuals in a society where human beings are able to preserve their a) Religion, b) Life, c) Intellect (reason), d) Family (descendants) and e) Property (wealth). Some scholars have added human dignity to the list. These are seen as indispensable to the survival and spiritual well-being of individuals and their impairment would bring harm to normal order in a society.
>
> 2. *Hajiyat* (required or complementary) - to help make human life easy on earth or things that concern the prevention of difficulty

among people. They are not in themselves essential, but they seek to protect and promote the essential benefits of individuals.

3. *Tahsiniyat* (embellishments or improvement) - in order to beautify human life. They seek to attain refinement and perfection in the customs and conduct of the people at all levels. The list of *hajiyat* and *Tahsiniyat* is endless.

This is not a place to elaborate the Islamic concept of rights, but it is interesting to note that these inalienable rights of individuals conform to Islam's concept of human beings as God's emissaries on earth. This is a wider concept, as nationality or citizenship is not purely bound by geographical boundaries in Islam.

Human beings struggled throughout history to secure their basic rights. But the results were often selective, i.e., the rights were confined to a few people of the elite or ruling class. Common people were generally denied their full civic and political rights and were burdened with duties only. Unfortunately, many 'third world' countries even today are run by dictatorial and tyrannical regimes and as such fail to give the basic rights to their own people. Also in many developed countries these rights are still discriminatory; often not including all the communities, especially the minority weaker people. Some communities in these countries, particularly the ones who fail to raise their voice or articulate their needs, are usually excluded. This inequality leads to social disharmony which in the end affects the whole of society.

Britain's anti-discrimination legislations are generally known to be stronger, but they do not include religious discrimination in public life. As a result, communities that identify themselves with faith suffer manifold discrimination. Only recently with the coming implementation of the European Employment Directives by the end of 2003, this will hopefully be redressed in the area of employment. But what about in other areas?

The concept of equal citizenship can only work when there

is public acceptance of all communities as legitimate and valued members of the society so that no community or group feels excluded and remain in the periphery. This acceptance brings natural respect for all communities and individuals within them. Respect is central to self-esteem and the sense of identity of an individual. Respect is also important for community confidence. In an inclusive society no community is subjected to offensive stereotypes and jokes or remarks, or viewed with suspicion, particularly by people in authority and the media. In addition, no community should face deliberate or unintended prejudice or discrimination.

Even without discrimination some communities or groups can suffer from political and socio-economic disadvantages for which they need support in capacity building so that they can exercise their legitimate rights as citizens. They not only need assurances but also opportunities to preserve their cultural identities.

People's basic rights and responsibilities, exercising of power, accountability and freedom are fundamental to any civil society. Only through the active participation, meaning active citizenship, of all in the society can we achieve these. Passive citizenship creates stagnation and gradual fossilisation of a community which then negatively affects the wider society. The following, if proactively pursued by all citizens, guarantee the success of a society:

Tolerance and understanding, valuing diversity and cultural differences

Mutual support

Mutual participation

Tackling harassment or violence

Programme to challenge preconceptions and stereotypes

Openness and cross-cultural contact

Breaking down ignorance and fear

Readiness to explore and resolve conflict

Using/teaching English language to empower people

The task of active citizenship is a challenge for all in society. However, it is the responsibility of those in authority to seriously try to engage and involve people from all communities in this endeavour. Their job is to create a proper social, economic and political environment so that every community feels comfortable in this engagement. At the same time, there should also be the opportunities to legally challenge things if they are not going in the proper direction or are hindered. The anti-discrimination legislation and the mechanism to challenge it should be easily available to all people.

Faith, Identity and Post-modernism

The Enlightenment in the eighteenth century set the scene for modernism that gave rise to rational thinking to solve scientific, economic, political and social questions. The scientific, industrial and now technological development opened a new door of opportunity for humanity. With them came economic prosperity as well as the political and social progress of people, mainly in the West. Modernism attempted to articulate the meaning of the natural world and social dynamics in terms of certain laws. In fact, by using human potential, modernism helped western societies to attain material prosperity. However, it arrogantly tried to create a conviction that human beings are the measure of everything, with their ability to solve all the problems in the world. Modernism has also brought the dilution of moral and ethical values and thus created divisions within humanity. The inequality between the first world with its mountainous wealth and power and the third world with its poverty, debt and disease is now undermining the peace and stability of the entire world.

Then, in the 1970s, emerged the concept of post-modernism with a different set of norms and values that is trying to define the future course of humanity. It tends to create a better world by promoting green movements and creating consciousness among people of food habits and healthy lifestyles. However, post-modernism maintains that there are no universal rules or values in the world, and so there is no absolute truth either. In short, post-modernism believes in relativism rather than reality, style rather than content and social fluidity rather than traditionalism. The idea of absolute identity, according to this concept, is a myth. With declining religious adherence and the breaking up of families, the media have taken the centre stage to provide human beings with an ever-changing identity. Those who own or run the media thus wield tremendous influence over human life.

In the Post-modernist approach identities are constantly changing. The belief of having one primary identity with a sense of certainty and reliability, as in the case of the traditional setting, does not hold. Post-modernism could, thus, lead human beings down the slippery slope of losing their identity altogether because of the negative effect by the dominant media run by a few profit-making individuals or groups of people.

The era of post-modernism, on the other hand, has weakened die-hard secularism or even atheism and brought a new consciousness about one's culture, faith and religion, albeit in a relativistic way. Features of globalisation have played an important part in this. Many individuals are now confident in their faith-based identity and many minority communities are capable of sustaining themselves as faith-based communities. In Britain, cultural practices, family values and religious rituals have now become features of a pluralist society and with numerous mosques, temples and other religious centres a new British landscape is in the making. The last two decades have seen a qualitative transformation of social norms and values in

Britain. While ethnic identity, gender and sexuality have become politicised in this period, faith identity has also gained ground, not only within the minority communities but also in the majority community as well. The issue of faith identity is now in the public domain.

This apparent competition of priority between ethnic and faith identity may have created some confusion regarding loyalty and allegiance of individuals in their social life. However, in reality, most individuals make sensible judgement as to which identity they will espouse at certain situations. Some may assert their geographic and ethnic identity at times of necessity when faced with pure racism, others prefer to emphasise their faith or religious identity when they encounter discrimination on the basis of religion. In the absence of any law protecting non-Christian religions there may be no mechanism of monitoring discrimination due to religion, but the message is now loud and clear that religion is a source of discrimination and religious identity is now a big issue.

However, depending on the type of challenges people face they use their single, dual or multiple identities. Individuals challenge prejudice and discrimination in their preferred method. With this social trend, it will now be more difficult to sideline religion from the public arena for long. The fact is that Islam and some other religions like Christianity espouse trans-ethnic identities, as they have within them many people of diverse racial and ethnic origin. And so faith identity should be seen as the natural expression of many people. Religious identity has thus become more relevant in modern Britain. Failure to acknowledge this can be hurtful to individuals and damaging to communities. This could harm community relations as well.

Economic and political factors also influence individual and community identity. Many individuals who belong to disadvantaged minorities use faith to withstand their difficulties. Although people in authority are reluctant to admit this, these people do not give up their struggle for the recognition of their faith identity. Muslims in particular, seem to be more conscious of their faith identity, as they are suffering from atrocities in many places because of their religion.

It is true that in the political and social context, identity is linked with allegiance and loyalty. In that respect multiple identities have multiple allegiances, for individuals and for communities. Confident individuals and respectful communities are well placed to navigate through their different shades of allegiance and loyalty without harming others or undermining their contract with a country. They know how to prioritise different aspects of their identities in certain situation. Whatever the influence of expediency or emotion in some people this prioritisation is in human nature. Thus, we see football players or supporters of a team behaving the way they behave to express their loyalty to the team as and when required. That does not mean they forego their other identities at that moment. Multiple identities are thus, not seen as problem at all. It is never a threat to a society, nor a state. It is not a matter of religion, nor an issue of *halal* or *haram*, to maintain different identities in tandem.

Now, let us see how the concept of a Muslim identity fits in with modern Britain and how it helps Muslims to become proactive in terms of their social responsibility.

10. MUSLIM IDENTITY & SOCIAL RESPONSIBILITY

Having a Muslim identity refers to the *Muslimness* of a person which has current expression and is being used to express how Muslims see themselves vis a vis others and in the society in which they live. Muslims are the largest minority religious group in Britain and, like Christians and some other religious groups, they are multi-racial and multi-cultural. There are black, brown and white Muslims across the country, although most of them are non-white and are concentrated in certain cities and regions. Although their encounter with Britain took place a long time ago and they have been living here as a community for many generations the recent debate on their identity and question of their loyalty by a section of the media and other establishments seem to be due to the new trend of Islamophobia. To many within the Muslim community this is patronising. General ignorance of religious and cultural differences on the one hand and over-politicisation of Islam throughout the world on the other have probably contributed to this situation.. People in authority are, unfortunately, ignoring the fact that Islam does not represent 'a rigid, fundamentalist, anti-western, anti-modernist religiosity'.[156]

What then, does the Muslim identity entail and how would it express itself in the complex, multicultural and post-modern Britain of today?

To get a broader idea of Muslim identity one has to see Islam's view of human beings vis-a-vis the world and the concept of universal nationhood or *ummah* in Islam. This has been discussed in Chapter 8.

Islam plays a meaningful and effective role in Muslim life in all ages and places. Vision and reality might have differed during different phases of history, but Islam's mission is to produce such global people who would work not for Muslims but also for the benefit of other peoples. When Muslims have put Islam in the right context, i.e., when it is no more a list of lifeless rituals with a dogmatic view of others, its dynamic and creative features have shaped Muslim life in a positive manner. As such, one's Muslimness revolves around his or her task in working for the good of all - in the family, neighbourhood and society. Muslims can never confine themselves to their own clan, tribe, race or even their ummah alone. The idea of narrow attachment to one's own people alone and considering others as 'them' or aliens is borne out of the *Jahiliyah,* that is pre-Islamic. The inflated tribal dignity of the past, the nationalistic arrogance of the early 20th century or the neo-fanaticism of religion or secularism of the present era cannot impress upon a Muslim.

As proponents of peace in the world and submission to one Lord, Muslims work for the universal good of human beings. They cannot subscribe to the concept of 'my nation, right or wrong', as this often unjustifiably sets one group of people against the other and destroys the fabric of society. Muslimness is thus a deeply embedded sense of consciousness and sub-consciousness that governs and prevails upon a Muslim's thoughts, behaviour and choices. Undiluted faith is essential to Muslims, in their personal as well as communal life. The concept of community feeling is integral in Islam and severing link with one's community is considered a major sin.

One's Muslim identity is deeply rooted in one's awareness of responsibility on earth and accountability to God for one's actions. As a community of moderation the Muslims' task of reminding themselves and others of their divine task on earth. Faith is, of course, at the core of Muslim identity which they need to contextualise in terms of time and space. Education plays a vital role in building this identity. Home, family and community are thus vital for Muslims, as they all contribute to building the Muslim character from the beginning. Once Muslims are equipped with these ingredients they can positively act and participate in any society.

The collective Muslim identity is as important as the individual one; the concept of the *ummah* or global Muslim community is paramount in Islam. Although Muslims lost their single geopolitical entity, since the second century of Islamic calendar they remain connected and unified in a common 'brotherhood' as a result of their common beliefs; the five pillars and overall allegiance to Islam. All these were rooted in the Qur'an and the *Sunnah*. The banner of this universal brotherhood was being upheld till the collapse of the Ottoman Khilafah, although towards the end it was only symbolic. Since then, sectarian and nationalistic chauvinism has weakened this sense of brotherhood, and now with their categorisation as 'moderate', 'extremist' and other classifications, Muslims feel more divided. However, their universal desire for allegiance to one *ummah* is still alive everywhere.

Muslim identity does not necessarily clash with one's ethnic, linguistic, geographical or other identity, whether on a macro or micro scale. In a genuinely pluralist society different aspects of a

Muslim's identity fit in and bring out a healthy outcome. Human beings' multifarious features include their sources of strength, which are seen as complementary, not competitive. As one's Muslim identity is based on the belief in the oneness of the human race, it subscribes to the progress and development of a common human destiny. One's ethnic, linguistic or racial identity on its own has the most likelihood of becoming biased or blinded, like the tribal identity of the pre-Islamic Arabia or the nationalistic identity of the modern era. As one's Muslim identity is linked with one's relationship with God and His creation, no Muslim can claim superiority over others, Muslims or non-Muslims. God alone knows who is superior on the basis of individual piety.[158] As no Muslim has the right to claim this superiority, no one can be in a position to display any arrogance.

Throughout Islamic history Muslims have generally tried to marry all aspects of identities in their contemporary societies and fuse them into one universal human identity. Muslims maintained this through the proper education and parenting of their new generations. Unfortunately, individuals such as Lord Macaulay (1800-59) deliberately wanted to undermine the identity of the Indian people by imposing an educational system 'to form a class who may be interpreters between us and the millions whom we govern – a class of persons, Indian in blood and colour, but English in task, in opinions, in morals and in intellect'.[159] As a result, Muslims who swallowed this pill of the colonial education system without thinking carefully became victims of an inferiority complex, perhaps because they could not change their colour and background, and perhaps because they could not absolutely abandon their Muslim identity.[160] Things were not dissimilar in other parts of the world ruled by other European countries. Muslims are now recuperating from this colonial legacy.

Muslimness in its height is linked with the confidence that genuine Muslims could be the rightful inheritors of their righteous and successful predecessors who proved themselves to be capable of great accomplishments and sacrifice for human beings - in artistic beauty, literary masterpieces, science, law, philosophy and other human areas. It implies a reluctance and opposition to submit to secular and amoral worldviews that undermines human dignity. Nor does the dictum of post-modern moral relativism has any place in Muslimness. Confident Muslims can never see the world in terms of 'us' and 'them'. They never subscribe to the arrogant 'holier than thou than' attitude towards others. What matters to them is justice, not vengeance, and righteousness, not self-righteousness.

Muslim identity brings courage and humility among Muslims, particularly its youth. It creates in them a positive Muslim personality.[161] It leads them to pro-active engagement with their brothers in humanity. They observe, reflect, admire and accept the positive and productive aspects of their surroundings. However, they keep away from the blind imitation of others, as they are aware that imitation can lead to a distortion in their identity creating a crisis within their personality. As long as Islam is understood properly, one's Muslim identity is guided by the spirit, and not merely by rituals of Islam. One can be a confident Muslim and at the same time be a British or Egyptian, Anglo-Saxon or Malay. Geographic nationality, race and language have never proved divisive in Islam, except during the final days of colonialism when many Arabs, Turks and Muslims of various geographical backgrounds adopted a narrow nationalism and fought one another only to bring about their own downfall. Needless to say, it was also a part of the colonial design of 'divide and rule' or 'divide and quit' policy.

Muslim identity is born of the open, transparent and dynamic nature of Islam as a universal religion. It is thus never closed or stagnant. The vibrancy of the Muslim identity catapults young Muslims to assert their active citizenship, i.e., respectful integration, which has been the hallmark of Muslim dynamism throughout history. No matter whether they live in a Muslim-majority or minority situation or whether they live in ease or difficulty, the Muslim identity always expects Muslims to be pro-active in their social contract as citizens of a country. The Prophet said, 'The best one among you is the best towards people'.[162]

Throughout history various communities, including Muslims in some places, which opted for ghettoisation because of fear or inflated pride lost out. Their reactive stance only brought about alienation for them in the society, and their seclusion helped fuel distrust and hatred. As a result, some of them faced 'ethnic cleansing' at a later stage. The 'Children of Israel' in Egypt, Muslims in Spain and Jews in Europe could be cited as archetypal cases. On the other hand, those who opted for assimilation in the 'melting pot' culture of dominant societies also faced total dissolution within a few generations. Like 'biological species' communities have become extinct as well.

Individual human beings have duties assigned to them by God instructing them as to how to lead their life on earth. At the same time, they take part in a contract with the country in which they have willingly decided to reside. As long as the former does not directly contradict with the latter and individuals play an active citizenship role in the society, there should be no reason for disharmony. Thus the natural demand of Muslimness or the Muslim identity is about playing one's full role as a human being on earth and citizen of a country. As servants of God Muslims feel part of the global humanity whether in the East or in the West, as the world is God's creation. At the same time, as citizens of a country they make an incessant effort to make positive contributions toward its material and moral development. In this age of moral relativism selfish Puritanism can be counter-productive to them.

The Muslim community in Britain has come to a stage when almost all British Muslims accept the need to become a respectable part of the British society so that they are able to participate fully in mainstream professions through education, employment, business, media and politics. To do otherwise would only serve to defeat their purpose as a community. It is encouraging that, in spite of many challenges, the picture is rapidly improving. More Muslims are now engaged in playing their rightful role in various sectors of society, including politics and the media. They are contributing to the mosaic of the new British pluralism and its multicultural heritage. The fact that Muslims now feel that they are 'Muslims *of* Britain' rather than 'Muslims *in* Britain', tells us how confident they feel about themselves and how much they have matured over the past decades. Due to the continuous interaction with mainstream society over the last decade or so the debate over the terms 'British Muslim' or 'Muslims of Britain' have become semantic. This optimism does not underrate the difficulties, challenges and barriers they are facing. This is a reality they have to face with dignity.

Without undermining or abandoning their root in faith and culture Muslims have been respectfully integrating, not assimilating, as a valued and integral part of the society. Integration entails interaction, participation and engagement with mutual respect and genuine autonomy. Integration means talking with, not talking to, other communities and sharing issues and concerns of commonality with them. Where integration is compared with social diffusion with others, assimilation is compared with dissolution. As a faith-based community Muslims, thus, cannot accept the slippery slope of assimilation and totally lose their identity.

The sustainable development and prosperity of a community is only guaranteed if they feel confident in their own cultural strengths and religious qualities. This strengthens the wider society as well. Muslims with their unique principles, values, community ethos and social etiquette not only survived in alien social environments but also progressed enormously in whatever they pursued. Muslim traders in the Far East and sub-Saharan Africa, even at times when they had little political power, could be cited as examples. Assertion is linked with power - material or moral-spiritual. In the peak of Muslim progress they were well equipped with both of them. Later on, as Muslims were gradually losing material power, moral-spiritual power remained the key to holding on to their influence. From the 18th century onwards the Muslim influence was shrinking and Europeans were asserting their position above others with, primarily, material power.

Assertion works when the community interacts and engages with others, in participation, not in isolation. In the case of the Muslim community in Britain, within which there are many newly-arriving communities, its first stage is to keep itself united and at the same time build bridges with others, learn from the experiences of other minority communities who are still struggling to make their root stronger in the new situation. On the other hand, they need to take part in the common affairs of all so that they work for a shared benefit, a common vision. Muslims have been asked in the Qur'an to work for the common good.[163] They cannot lock themselves, ghettoised, in a small world.

An important question may arise as to how long a community remains an immigrant community in a country. This depends on the social dynamics of both the new and the older communities. It depends on how fast the new community settles, and starts its interaction and engagement with the wider society along with maintaining its heritage. At the same time, it also depends on the readiness of the wider society to accept it as (equal partner)?. For Muslims who have many indigenous people in their fold, the issue is not straightforward.

Some Muslims may advocate an isolationist approach for fear that the non-Muslim environment would endanger their faith and the fabric of their community. This is an over-reaction and the majority of Muslims never adopted this path. Prophet Muhammad was himself living with his small community in the midst of Makkan pagans and he did not leave Makkah until it became unbearable for him and his small community. A significant section of the Muslim *ummah* has been living as minority citizens for centuries in countries such as India, China and Russia. However, Muslims should not voluntarily reside in a country where they are forced to act against their faith or are unable to fulfil their basic religious duties. In most western countries there would hardly be any region now that would allow this to happen. Muslims may face difficulties in some non-Muslim countries; they are facing persecution in many Muslim-majority countries. In those situations Muslims need to get their heads together and work hard to overcome any difficulties.

Muslims conduct themselves in the spirit of their faith, as the most important duty of Muslims is to create awareness, bearing witness[164] to God's message among people. This is done through their individual action as well as social dealings, traditions, customs, behaviour and etiquette. Prophets and other morally upright people succeeded in winning over the hearts of people through righteousness and justice. People dislike bigotry or self-righteousness.

The theological debate of *halal* and *haram* for Muslims in residing in a Muslim-minority country has to be seen in context. Islam does not list all *halal* things; it has a list of a few *haram* things and the rest of the world is *halal* for Muslims provided, of course, that they have a good intention preceding any action. Muslims have to be aware that any social activities that do not contradict Islamic principles are acceptable.

Muslims, therefore, do not have to be extra worried in being part of a non-Muslim society where citizenship rights and opportunities are available for all and where they can practise their faith without fear. As long as they are able to protect their Islam and can continue to live as a community they should not have a problem in those societies. Of course, there are issues with every society and they need to be addressed by all in it. In pluralist societies hostilities and antagonism can be avoided if conventions of politeness and common sense are ensured, especially to protect the susceptible minority communities. As Muslims are enjoined to care for human beings, creatures and the environment, they find such participation in society rewarding in life. Muslims have a unique role to play in any society they decide to reside in.

Now here comes the issue of Britishness *vis a vis* Muslimness. Are they in conflict with each other? Given the historical evolution of the British society, especially after the Second World War, Britishness has evolved into something more diverse and pluralistic. The emergence of multicultural pluralism has contributed to its nature. Migrant communities have settled and the dynamics in community relations has transformed. Muslims have lived in Britain for a few generations as a community and have also attracted some converts from the indigenous people. As a result, 'the prospect of communities finding a better, more just and humane way of living together has improved in the recent past'.[165] Britishness now subscribes to the demographic reality of Britain with white, brown and black people on the one hand and Christians, Jews, Muslims and other religious groups on the other. Muslims, like other minority communities, have a role to play in bringing this pluralist nature of Britishness into fruition. In a positive social environment there should be no dichotomy between one's Muslimness or Christianness, and Britishness. However, one has to be clear that Britishness is not the same as Englishness, which is linked to one racial group, nor Christianness which is linked to one religion.

There is, however, an issue of historical legacy. Due to Britain's colonial past non-white people or probably non-Christians still consider the term 'Britishness' non-inclusive. Some of the white British community may also be unwilling to accept non-whites in their fold. This is the reality in some people's mindset even today. Thus we see the practical barriers against social inclusion in day-to-day British life. 'Britishness, as much as Englishness, has systematic, largely unspoken, racial connotations'.[166] There are still rightist elements in the society that feed into the ideal of an exclusive nature for Britishness. Some people still use Britishness and Englishness interchangeably. Here, political culture and race have been intertwined. Britain's recent pro-American foreign policy *vis a vis* Muslim world has also contributed to the negative feelings about Britishness.

Some Muslims ask the seemingly genuine but rather naïve question of whether they are bound by the constitution of a non-Muslim country that allows interest, the consumption of alcohol and other things that are contrary to the teachings of Islam. They forget that the world is not a perfect place and many Muslim countries themselves are engaged in similar things. The question one has to answer is: are Muslims obliged to turn to such activities? If the answer is no, then there is no reason why Muslims should fail to respect the constitutional and legal framework of the country in which they have decided to settle. In fact, in any constitutional framework there is room for the conscience clause, that a citizen has the right to conscientious objection and to withdraw from certain acts because of religious or ethical reason. Parents have the right to choose their children's schools or withdraw them from certain classes in school. There may be some cost in this, but conscientious people stick to their principles even if they have to suffer. Prophet Yusuf preferred prison rather than living freely in sin and said, 'prison is better than committing injustice'.[16] Those who refused to join in the American government's unjust war in Vietnam opted for this conscience clause.

It is unfortunate that the Muslim assertion of a faith-based identity has created a myth that Muslims are unwilling to be an active part of the British society. The historical misunderstanding of Muslims in Europe and the recent wave of Islamophobia across the Atlantic are feeding into this feeling. Islam is regarded by some as a religion that does not fit in well with the post-modern pluralistic vision of society. Nothing is further from the truth. Unfortunately, Muslims are also partly to blame for this, as a small section of them show disregard for other religions and tend to adhere to a belligerent and intolerant attitude toward other people. As a result, Muslims are mistakenly classified as liberals, moderates and radicals. This fits in with the distorted views that are currently being aired in the media, views which seem to revel in depicting practising Muslims as fanatics or extremists. Whatever the reason for this, this classification of Muslims or any other people for egotistic or political reasons does not help in strengthening community harmony and pluralism.

There is suspicion from all sides due to ignorance and a lack of understanding. On the one hand, the white British community fear that diversity will bring a loss of nostalgic golden European identity, and on the other, some Muslims go further in reminiscing of their golden days and only dream of their past. It is time that everyone works for the present and realises that Islam is a religion of peace, justice and compassion. The fact of the matter is, there is no room for fanaticism and dogmatism in Islam and there is no coercion in it either.[168]

Islam has given utmost importance to knowledge and education. Muslims are asked to pray for their increase in knowledge and understanding.[169] In fact, true faith is inconceivable without it. Understanding the text as well as the context is thus vital for a Muslim. Prophet Muhammad laid great emphasis on it when he declared that 'seeking knowledge is compulsory for every Muslim, man and woman'.[170] He said that a knowledgeable person is far superior to a general worshipper: *'The superior rank of a scholar in relation to the worshipper is like my superior rank in relation to the lowest of my companions'*.[171] Ali ibn Abi Talib, the wise companion of Prophet Muhammad and the fourth rightly-guided caliph in Islam, mentioned in a poem that a knowledgeable person is immortal.[172]

The concept of assuming an identity based on knowledge and understanding makes Muslims comfortable and confident in their position in the society. It is encouraging to note that many amongst the new generation of Muslim youth are now getting more and more confident about their role in building a fair and just society in pluralist Britain.

II. MUSLIM IDENTITY: CHALLENGES
AND OPPORTUNITIES

We live in a world today where Muslims as a faith community face a lot of challenges, internal as well as external and local as well as global. In recent times, from the Rushdie affair in 1989 to the occupation of Iraq, Muslims as a whole have been at the receiving end of prejudice, discrimination and hate from many quarters. On the other hand, the feeling of impotence, tension and frustration is widespread among them. As part of the global *ummah* all these issues haunt every conscious Muslim wherever they are and they impact on their thought process and personality.

Global events are however beyond the control of ordinary Muslims. The factors that affect the day-to-day life of individual Muslims in a country are more important. It is a worry that with each succeeding generation of Muslims in Britain a section is assimilating into the prevailing dominant British culture. Some of them follow their peers in drinking, wining and dating. A small section is engaged in drugs, gang-fighting and other criminal behaviour. There are also instances of promiscuous sexual practices among a small section. Although in the wider society these issues do not make any moral uproar any more, except by people who see them as socially and economically costly, they are issues of principles for Muslims. Muslims feel appalled when they find that many social diseases are creeping into their community and are resulting in domestic violence and family breakdown.

Then there is a general decline in religious adherence among many in the Muslim community, e.g., in five daily prayers, attending mosque services and fasting in Ramadan. Although there is no hard data available, it is thought that 'at least 80% of European Muslims do not, for example, perform their daily prayers. Less than 40% attend the Friday gathering at the mosque. About 70%, however, do fast during the sacred month of Ramadan'.[173] At the same time, how many of those who practise their religion look into the spirit of those practices? It is an irony that, in spite of all the challenges before them, some Muslims are still engrossed in apathy and indifference in the affairs that affect them. The general level of ignorance is also another factor that threatens the Muslim position in a society.

On the other side of the spectrum, there is an element of sad fatalism among Muslims. Some are struggling to retain their 'purity' of religion by segregating themselves from the wider society. For them religious observance means seclusion and *ghettoisation*. As a result of their lack of confidence, they take interaction and integration as assimilation. They seem to live in perpetual fear of others, including probably non-practising Muslims, thinking that the society around them is conspiring to contaminate their piety. Then, there are Muslims who have little knowledge of their surroundings and they do not bother about it. Their one-dimensional view of life cannot see the nature of Islam's universality and its resilience in time and space. Some within this trend even see other Muslims with suspicion and hold extreme views about them. Intolerance and often extremism put them on the media spotlight and some unfortunately thrive on this publicity. Some of these Muslims are seen as active, but unfortunately they are busy 'converting the already converted' and are in the process of competing, not complementing, with other Muslims. Perhaps this type of activism come out of sincerity or concern and passion for the *ummah*, but because of the lack of broader knowledge and contextual understanding of Islam it harms the image of Islam at the end. There seems to be varied degree of self-righteousness in them which ordinary people, Muslims and non-Muslims alike, feel negative about.

The generation gap between the older and the younger Muslims, in terms of cultural and social practices, career choices and lifestyles, is another concern which is on the increase. At the same time, the debate over some aspects of Islamic jurisprudence and contextual application of Islam in the modern world is also getting prominence among Muslims. The trend among some Muslim youth, even those who are ostentatiously practising and known to be active in the field of Islam, in their dress, shape of beard, make up and appearance invites eyebrows from the elders. The influence of libertine lifestyle and consumerism is having its toll on many younger Muslims. As social diseases are spreading unabated young people from all communities are being affected.

While Muslims are passing their days with a feeling of global injustice upon them and trying to address their internal challenges, the reality of daily suspicion and discrimination is giving rise to their frustration, especially among the youth. There is now a growing feeling in the Muslim community that their human rights and civil liberties are being bypassed in many western countries, including Britain, after September 11. Whether rigidly practising or 'liberalised Muslims' or even the middle-path followers of Islam, Muslims are facing the brunt of Islamophobia from many quarters and in different ways. Islam, the religion of peace, has indeed a bad image. This may affect their journey to a genuine integration with mainstream society.

It is probably true that the pressure on British Muslims *vis a vis* race and faith hate is not as severe as in some other countries, say in post-September 11 America. Muslims in Britain generally have no difficulty in observing the major Islamic practices, such as prayer in workplaces or educational institutions. The British Foreign Office has been arranging remarkable service facilities for the British pilgrims in Saudi Arabia for the last few years. Like other citizens, including those in the faith communities, they can build religious centres, such as mosques and Islamic centres and organise themselves in organisations and associations, locally and nationally. They can wear *hijab* and avail *halal* meat, although there has arisen a serious debate over the latter. They can avail equal opportunities in education, housing and employment. They can own properties and have access to legal protection in many areas of life, including the right to appeal to the law. In spite of many institutional weaknesses Muslims are generally enjoying the benefit of Britain's emerging pluralism.

Many Muslim youth in Britain are also now showing an increasing level of maturity and dignity in dealing with their emotions, anger and frustration at the cycle of events in Muslim lands. There may be provocative outbursts from some frustrated fringe elements, but it looks like the community as a whole is gradually gaining more confidence in coping with feelings borne out of external factors. They are gradually learning to articulate their principled views on say the occupation of Muslim lands and usurpation of their wealth. They have realised that their strength lies

in strengthening their communities through education, employment, business and other entrepreneurial ventures in the midst of a
pluralist Britain. This is slowly paying dividends.

The Muslim community in Britain has come a long way in its
achievements list as well. In spite of their weaknesses, limitations
and social constraints, their struggle to create some infra-structure
through the establishment of mosques, Islamic centres, schools,
halal food, etc, is an encouraging phenomenon. These are the
products of dedication, perseverance and love for their religion by
the majority of Muslims. With hard work, enterprise and strong
community feeling they have brought a new look in the British
landscape and enhanced its pluralistic nature. If only these proud
contributions were well coordinated they would have more national impact.

Although the situation is far from perfect, a new vibrant and
dynamic Muslim community is now emerging in Britain. More
women are now choosing to wear *hijab*, more men are willingly
sporting beards and are becoming more assertive about them as
symbols of their identity. People are taking more care in gaining knowledge about Islam, Muslim history, other people and the
contemporary world. Even secular minded Muslims are now ask-
ing 'what' and 'how' of Islam, rather than 'why' of it. In education, community work, politics, media, relief and charity there
is new enthusiasm, energy and awareness among the youth.
Mosques are now gradually reclaiming their original role of being
a community hub for people of all backgrounds, in line with the
example of the Prophet's mosque in Madinah. The under-repre-
sented groups within the Muslim community, the young people
and women, are now starting to play some of their rightful roles
in an increasing number of mosques and Islamic centres. More
home-grown and English speaking Imams, some from the sec-

ond generation, are now leading prayers and giving sermons in the mosques. Many professional young people are taking up important places in the public arena. Although a European Muslim identity is in its infancy the sign of a more positive Muslim culture seems to be on the horizon in Britain.

Muslim youth are no longer meek or invisible. They are conscious about racism and Islamophobia and getting more assertive in dealing with these social scourges. For most of them their Muslim identity supersedes ethnic identity and they find no contradiction in various aspects of their identity. Some may join Islamic groups just because of the negative image of Islam, but most are becoming serious about their positive role in the society as Muslims. Most Muslim organisations are now politically and financially independent of Middle Eastern influence, unlike in their predecessors' time. Many of them have learnt the skills to tap regeneration money from various government and European funding sources. Muslim representation in various statutory and voluntary bodies, locally and nationally, is slowly increasing and good partnership is emerging in some sectors. With the successful incorporation of a religious question in Census 2001 Muslims, like many other faith communities, are now confident that their case for a proper representation and funding allocation will now be stronger. This has a huge political and social implication for the religious identity of all the faith communities.

Although Muslim children are still under performing in the GCSE exams and are very much behind in the job market, the young Muslims are generally better educated and better employed than their elders. They are more conscious about their rights and responsibilities and they expect a respected and recognised position in the society.

In this state of affairs, the Muslim community has to build on their successes and remain strong and united in these challenging times. They have to maintain their middle-path approach in terms of their religious and cultural practices. Even in the event of provocation they have to realise that moderation is the spirit of Islam and is fundamentally important for Muslims, particularly in a pluralist society. It is true that moderation has a penalty; it does not attract attention from others or the media. But at the end it is the only Islamic way to success. Islam's position on extremism is clear.[174] Muslims are expected to choose the spirit of Islam rather than its lifeless rituals, action rather than rhetoric and enterprise rather than dogmatism in their life. Just a label of religion without substance is not helpful to anyone. As an individual, every Muslim should look into the dynamic personality of Prophet Muhammad and as a community they must remain focused on their purpose. Young Muslims need positive role models and there are now quite a good number in the community. It is expected that these successful people encourage others by example.

As justice is at the heart of Islam,[175] Muslims do not condone any unprincipled or unjust method to achieve even a just cause. Islam's justice is unilateral and it is neither selective nor time-bound. This spirit of justice and moderation in all affairs of life should be the essence of Muslim passion to work for the betterment of all.

Building bridges among people and communities and creating good community relations are at the root of Islam's social life. Muslims are expected to excel in them in order to create a safer and better society. Despair, disaffection and grievances should not lead them to adopt policies and actions that go against the public interest. Muslims should not only confine themselves for their own welfare but also for the welfare of all – in education, employment, housing, health and other sectors of life. They should be in the forefront of their social responsibility toward others and they need to work hard toward creating structures for and building capacities among people so that weaker individuals and communities can participate equally in the wider society. At the same time, they need to work with others for a violence-free civil society.

As a community grows with families and neighbourhoods, i.e., with people of different backgrounds, a Muslims duties and obligation toward others, be they Muslim or non-Muslim, are embedded in their religion. These duties and responsibilities[176] can only be effectively delivered in an environment of communal harmony. As such, Muslims are required to work for good community relations. Needless to say that similar covenants were also sent to the previous people.[177]

Muslims take their guidance from the life of Prophet Muhammad who was a perfect example of a community person, even before he became a Prophet. He was known as the *'Amin'* (trustworthy) and *'Sadiq'* (truthful) among the people of his city. He helped people in their need and mediated in their feud. When he received the first revelation and rushed home with anxiety and fear, his wife consoled him with the words that testified his service to the community. *'Never! By Allah, Allah will never disgrace you. You keep good relations with your kith and kin, help the poor and the destitute, serve your guests generously and assist the deserving calamity-afflicted ones'.*[178]

The Muslim responsibility toward their neighbours and other people in the community is mentioned in many Prophetic traditions as well. As a result, Muslims have taken these Qur'anic and Prophetic instructions of creating and maintaining good relationship with neighbours and others in humanity as their religious obligation. This has got such prominence in their mindset that Muslims, whether practising or not, try their best to remain good neighbours in all situations.

As the social inclusion agenda gains momentum, Muslims and some other faith communities are becoming aware that in an attempt to strive for inclusion in the dominant society, minority communities may weaken their attachment with their religious, cultural and traditional values. Many in the community fear that under the impact of marginalisation and demand to conform to the prevailing social norms they may lose their balance and harmony between this world and the hereafter. There is also a worry that, as a result of this social pressure, some in their community may develop distrust in themselves and other people through 'self-hate', violence and hypersensitivity; others may give in to fatalism and become despondent. This may dilute the spirit of their community feeling at some stage. This negative scenario could be true for others communities. Unless properly addressed by all, any marginalized community could create problems not only for themselves but also for the wider society.

Attempts for inclusion and community harmony can only succeed when they are a two way process. When the mainstream society shows empathy and respect to the minority communities and try to accommodate them as equal partners, the latter would feel confident and try to work together in the best possible manner. Whatever the social environment, the choice for Muslims is simple. As a community with a firm belief in the 'unity in diversity' of humankind[179] it is their divine task to proactively engage in building a harmonious society with others. As young people have the vitality, creativity, innovation and adventure to bring any social change, Muslim youth have thus a monumental task ahead. They can be the catalyst of a positive change in the future of the whole society. It is not surprising that most of the companions of Prophet Muhammad were between the age of 10 and 35.

As Islam has no hierarchical structure the responsibility of this positive social engagement lies with every Muslim. The nature of Islam is such that Muslims cannot be individualists, whether passive or greed-driven entrepreneurs. Muslims are required to be sociable, equipped with dynamism and public interest-driven entrepreneurship. As successes of individuals and a community are intertwined, Islam demands from its followers to be proactive social entrepreneurs. Parents, community elders and Imams play a vital role in producing this type of young people in the community. However, they all have to be armed with the knowledge and understanding of their own roots and of the contemporary society. In Islam there is no clash between tradition and modernity. The challenge for conscientious Muslims is to blend them into their individual and social life.

CONCLUSION

The debate surrounding human beings' racial or ethnic identity on the one hand and faith or religious identity on the other is as old as the formation of human societies on earth. The former is linked with one's ancestral origin and thus immutable, and the latter is a matter of choice. In any community race, religion, language and historical legacy produce a certain culture that influences individual identity. This cultural identity reflects many aspects of one's communal life.

In Islam, race, ethnicity and language of people are taken as a colourful mosaic and thus a matter of celebration. As God has given freewill to human beings Islam has valued diversity in a society. Those who have chosen Islam as their religion take Muslim identity seriously, without of course undermining their other aspects of identity. Their ability to define themselves is, in fact, the liberation of their intellect. This has made Muslims confident about their faith identity. This confidence not only enhances their participation in the social, economic and political life of their countries of residence but also encourages them to contribute something of value to the society in which they live. This is the true

Muslim manner, as Muslims were never meant to be a cocooned community. They can never remain in ghettos and spend their time agitating from the periphery.

At the same time, due to ignorance of Islam by non-Muslims and even some Muslims, and serious gaps in understanding about Muslim culture many, particularly secular minded people, fail to comprehend why faith identity is taken so seriously by Muslims and some other people. Fortunately, this gap of understanding is gradually narrowing.

As a result of the rapid expansion of the mass media, internet communications, immigration and asylum seeking, tourism and other factors, human societies see the daily manifestation of racial, cultural and religious multiplicity. Interconnectedness of societies has now become a feature of modernity, especially in the last few decades. People can now see themselves in the midst of many. They do not want to be assimilated if that means adopting the culture, religion, spiritual orientation, lifestyles or family patterns of the dominant group. People of reason know that differentiated and multi-level participation is essential for community harmony. A plurality of identity, from family to religion and from local community to nation state, is thus getting more recognition and taken more seriously.

It is true we live in an increasingly 'shrinking' world where human behaviour is influenced by many global forces. The impact of globalisation is now far reaching and swift, in social and other areas of human life. However, most of globalisation at this period of history is the images, artefacts and identities of western societies, including Japan. People in the poorer and weaker world are at the receiving end and they are evidently worried about this.

At the same time, in the post-modern world humanity is unfortunately more divided than ever, by racial or ethnic bigotry on the one hand and religious intolerance and fanaticism on the other. The new world order ushered by the fall of the Berlin wall is, instead of bringing hope to humanity, seemingly creating more divisions among various people in the world. Since then many people around the world have been going through more fear, death and destruction. The deterioration of civil liberty, human rights and freedom of expression on the pretext of 'war against terror' or 'national interest' in some powerful countries is a cause for concern for all of us. With powerful countries flexing their muscles with open attempts to bypass international norms, the poorer and weaker nations feel more vulnerable. Human rights groups are also worried about the effects of double standards in implementing international justice.

Ironically, it is not only the divisions between the West and the East or the North and the South which are on the increase, but also many societies are torn by divisions within themselves. Social exclusions and under-performance of many communities, even in the developed countries of the West like Britain, are fracturing community harmony, in spite of good attempts from many people.

Individuals and communities thus have a serious task ahead. When individuals are equipped with non-dogmatic faith and a broader vision of life they give rise to spiritual wealth which in turn strengthens their resolve for peace and justice in society. Faith not only brings solace to human hearts, but confidence in one's identity and heritage. It not only helps them to get closer to God but also to fight against their inner evils and get closer to people. When people of non-dogmatic faith join hands to work together for a common cause it then creates hope and optimism not only in them but also in the wider society.

All communities need to increase their understanding of one

another so that prejudice and hatred borne out of ignorance and fear of others are minimised or rooted out. This can only be possible by acknowledging and respecting the values and culture of all the communities and through interactive dialogue and engagement with one another. With the robust method of implementing equality of opportunity and strong legal apparatus to deal with discrimination, communities feel more hopeful and confident. Newer communities like those of the Muslims can gain more through hope and confidence.

In general terms, where there is faith there is hope. Muslims constitute about 3% of the British population and with a higher proportion of young people in the community they are now a significant and visible minority in Britain. A positive faith identity will definitely give Muslims confidence and conviction to work for the good of the wider society.

NOTES

1. Solomos, J., (1993), *Race and Racism in Britain*, pp. 58–59, Macmillan Press Ltd, London.

2. The Local Inter Faith Guide, (1999), *The Inter Faith Network for the UK*.

3. The Parekh Report, (2000), *The Future of Multi-Ethnic Britain: Report of the Commission on the Future of Multi-Ethnic Britain*, Profile Books Ltd.

4. The Runnymede Trust and the Uniting Britain Trust, *Response by the Commission on British Muslims and Islamophobia to the draft Code of Practice issued for Consultation by the Commission for Racial Equality*, (2002).

5. *The Guardian*, March 29, 2004

6. *The Guardian*, March 16, 2004

7. http://www.mcb.org.uk/Imamletter-31March04.pdf.

8. Qur'an 2:30, 6:166.

9. From Census 2001 information from the Office for National Statistics, the General Register Office for Scotland and the Northern Ireland Statistics and Research Agency.

10. *Encyclopaedia Britannica*, Copyright 1994-1999.

11. Qur'an 49:13.

12. *Encyclopaedia Britannica*, Copyright 1994-1999.

13. Panikos Panayi, (1994), *Immigration, Ethnicity and Racism in Britain 1815-1945*, p. 76, Manchester University Press.

14. Wirth, L., *The Problem of Minority Groups*, p. 347, in R. Linton (Ed.),

(1945), *The Science of Man in the World Crisis*, Columbia University Press, New York.

15. *Encyclopaedia Britannica*, Copyright 1994-1999.

16. *Rudyard Kipling's* (1885-1926) *Verse*, p. 320, 1928, Macmillan, London.

17. From *'I have a Dream'* speech from Encarta '99.

18. Eric Williams, (1964), *Capitalism and Slavery*, p. 7, Andre Deutsch, London.

19. Jeremy Black, (Ed.), (1999), *Encyclopaedia of World History*, p. 128, Paragon.

20. Ibid, p. 129.

21. Jackson, J. A., (1963), *The Irish in Britain*, pp. 7-11, Routledge, London.

22. Solomos, J., (1993), *Race and Racism in Britain*, p. 43, Macmillan Press Ltd, London.

23. Ibid, p. 47.

24. Gainer, B., (1972), *The Alien Invasion: the Origins of the Aliens Act of 1905*, Heinemann, London.

25. Solomos, J., (1993), *Race and Racism in Britain*, p. 47, Macmillan Press Ltd, London.

26. Dilip Hiro, (1992), *Black British, White British: A History of Race Relations in Britain*, p. 97, Paladin, London.

27. Ibid, p. 107.

28. Harris, C. (1988), *Images of Blacks in Britain*: 1930-60, in S. Allen and M. Macey (Eds), *Race and Social Policy*, p. 18, Economic and Social Research Council, London.

29. K. Lunn (Ed.), *Regulating the Reserve Army: Arabs, Blacks and the Local State in Cardiff*, 1919-45, in *Race and Labour in Twentieth Century Britain*, pp. 7-74, Frank Cass, London.

30. Solomos, J., (1993), *Race and Racism in Britain*, pp50-51, Macmillan Press Ltd, London,.

31. *Census* 2001.

32. Ibid, pp. 58-59.

33. Ibid, pp. 63-64.

34. Rose, E.J.B. et al. (1969), *Colour and Citizenship: A Report on British Race Relations*, p. 229, Oxford University Press.

35. Foot, P., (1965), *Immigration and Race in British Politics*, p. 44, Penguin Books.

36. Dilip Hiro, (1992), *Black British, White British: A History of Race*

Relations in Britain, Paladin, London.

37. Solomos, J., (1993), *Race and Racism in Britain*, P66, Macmillan Press Ltd, London.

38. *The Observer*, 21 April 1968.

39. Macdonald, I., (1983) *Immigration Law and Practice in the United Kingdom*, pp. 25-30, Butterworths.

40. Ibid, p. 69.

41. Jenkins, R. (1967), *Racial Equality in Britain*, in Anthony Lester (Ed.), Essays and Speeches by Roy Jenkins, p. 267, Collins: London.

42. Home Office, (1975). *Racial Discrimination*, Cmnd 6234, HMSO, London.

43. Solomos, J., (1993), *Race and Racism in Britain*, (1993), p88, Macmillan Press Ltd, London.

44. Swann, Lord Michael (1985), *Education for All: Report of the Committee of Inquiry into the Education of Children from Ethnic Minority Groups*, p5, Cmnd 9453, HMSO: London.

45. Ibid, p. 7.

46. Dilip Hiro, (1992), *Black British, White British: A History of Race Relations in Britain*, Paladin.

47. Ouseley, H. (1990), *Resisting Institutional Change,* in W. Ball and J. Solomos, (Eds), *Race and Local Politics*, Macmillan, Basingstoke.

48. Scarman, Lord, (1981), *The Brixton Disorders*, 10-12 April 1981: *Report of an Inquiry* by Rt. Hon. The Lord Scarman OBE, p. 135, HMSO, London.

49. Ibid, p. 64.

50. Laura Panketh, (2000), *Tackling Institutional Racism: Anti-racist Policies and Social Work Education and Training*, p. 21, The Policy Press.

51. Paul Foot, (1965), *Immigration and Race in British Politics*, p129, Penguin Books (cited from Sir Cyril Osborne, a Conservative MP)

52. Qur'an 7:12.

53. Aspects of Britain: *Ethnic Minorities*, (1991), p13, HMSO, London.

54. Ibid, p. 74.

55. Modood et al, (1997), *Ethnic Minorities in Britain: Diversity and Disadvantage, The Fourth National survey of Ethnic Minorities*, p. 273, Policy Studies Institute, London.

56. Ibid, p. 277.

57. Ibid, p. 279.

58. The Guardian, 12 March 2002.

59. Social Focus on Ethnic Minorities – A Publication of the

Government Statistical Service, (1996), p. 34, HMSO: London.

60. Ibid, p. 37.

61. Ibid, p. 46.

62. Modood et al, (1997), *Ethnic Minorities in Britain: Diversity and Disadvantage*, The Fourth National survey of Ethnic Minorities, Policy Studies Institute, London.

63. *Aspects of Britain: Ethnic Minorities*, (1991), p47, HMSO: London.

64. Solomos, J., (1993), *Race and Racism in Britain*, p. 107, Macmillan Press Ltd, London.

65. Richard Hatcher, (1995), *Racism in Children's Culture*, p. 97, in *Antiracism, Culture and Social Justice in Education*, (Eds), Griffiths M and Tonya, B., Trentham Books.

66. Prince Charles in his introduction to 'Roots of the Future', Commission for Racial Equality, 1996.

67. David Mason, (2000), *Race and Ethnicity in Modern Britain*, p. 31, Oxford University Press.

68. *The Guardian,* February 14, 2003 (from Census 2001).

69. *The Independent*, 22 April 2003.

70. Bhikhu Parekh in *The Independent*, 19 June 1996.

71. Qur'an 49:11.

72. Steve Bruce, (1995), *Religion in Modern Britain*, p. ix, Oxford University Press.

73. Qur'an 3:19.

74. Qur'an 2:2.

75. Qur'an 10:100.

76. *I Cor.* 12:8-9.

77. Rumman Ahmed and James Salter, (1999), *Ethnic and Faith Community Development*, p. 15, The Royal Borough of Kensington and Chelsea.

78. Ibid, p. 15.

79. The Parekh Report, (2000), *The Future of Multi-Ethnic Britain: Report of the Commission on the Future of Multi-Ethnic Britain*, p. 27, Profile Books Ltd.

80. Martin Henig, (1994), *Religion in Roman Britain in A History of Religion in Britain*, p. 13, (Eds. Sheridan Gilley W. J. Sheils), Blackwell.

81. Ibid, p. 23.

82. Bruce, (1995), *Religion in Modern Britain*, p. 3, Oxford University Press.

83. *Encyclopaedia of World History*, (2000), p. 68, (Ed. Professor Jeremy Black), Parragon, UK.

84. Syed Ameer Ali, (1926), *A Short History of the Saracens*, p. 321, Kitab Bhavan, New Delhi.

85. Ibid, pp. 327-329.

86. *Encyclopaedia of World History*, (2000), p. 25, (Ed. Professor Jeremy Black), Parragon, UK.

87. Ibid, pp. 356-357.

88. Ibid, p. 286.

89. Ibid, p. 288.

90. Ibid, p.120.

91. Ibid, p. 156.

92. Paul Badham, (1994), *Religious Pluralism in Modern Britain*, p. 488, (Eds. Sheridan Gilley W. J. Sheils), A History of Religion in Britain, Blackwell.

93. *The Local Inter Faith Guide*, (1999), The Inter Faith Network for the UK.

94. From *Census* 2001 Information from the Office for National Statistics, the General Register Office for Scotland and the Northern Ireland Statistics and Research Agency.

95. *The Muslim News*, 28 February 2003.

96. www.mcb.org.uk/Census2001.pdf.

97. Ibid, p. 90.

98. Monitoring Minority Protection in the EU: *The Situation of Muslims in the UK*, Open Society Institute, p. 72, 2002.

99. The Runnymede Trust and the Uniting Britain Trust, *Response by the Commission on British Muslims and Islamophobia to the draft Code of Practice* issued for Consultation by the Commission for Racial Equality, (2002).

100. Paul Badham, (1994), *Religious Pluralism in Modern Britain*, p. 497, (Eds. Sheridan Gilley W. J. Sheils), A History of Religion in Britain, Blackwell.

101. Qur'an 4:1, 10:19.

102. Qur'an 2:30, 6:166.

103. Qur'an 7:23.

104. Qur'an 2:34.

105. Qur'an 30:30.

106. Qur'an 91:8.

107. *Sahih Bukhari, Muslim* and others.

108. Qur'an 2:256, 10:99.

109. Qur'an 17:70, 2:29.

110. Qur'an 31:20.

111. Qur'an 7:17.

112. Qur'an 2:38, 13:7.

113. Qur'an 2:213, 5:48.

114. Qur'an 30:20, 30:22, 4:1, 49:13.

115. Qur'an 30:22.

116. Qur'an 49:10.

117. Qur'an 49:13.

118. *Bukhari and Muslim.*

119. *Abu Dawud* and *Tirmidhi.*

120. Qur'an 3:103.

121. Qur'an 21:92, 23:52.

122. Muhammad Asad, (1980), *The Message of the Qur'an*, p. 177, Dar al-Andalus, Gibralter.

123. Qur'an 2:143.

124. Qur'an 3:110.

125. Qur'an 3:103.

126. Qur'an 49:10.

127. *Bukhari*

128. *Bukhari*

129. Hamid Enayet, (1982), *Modern Islamic Political Thought*, p. 39, Austin: University of Texas Press.

130. Abdullah al-Ahsan, (1992), *Ummah or Nation: Identity Crisis in Contemporary Muslim Society*, p. 30, The Islamic Foundation, Leicester.

131. Hans Kohn, (1929), *A History of Nationalism in the East*, p. 8, New York Harcourt.

132. Bernard Lewis, (1967), *The Middle East and the West*, p. 70, Bloomington: Indiana University Press.

133. *Muslims in Britain*, (2002), Foreign and Commonwealth Office, London.

134. J. Sherif in *The Quest for Sanity: Reflections on September 11 and the Aftermath*, (2002), p. 163, Muslim Council of Britain.

135. Ibid, p. 164.

136. Ibid, p. 165.

137. Ibid, p. 167.

138. Philip Lewis, (2000), *Islamic Britain: Religion, Politics and Identity*

among British Muslims, p. 11, I. B. Tauris Publishers.

139. J. Sherif in *The Quest for Sanity: Reflections on September 11 and the Aftermath*, (2002), p. 169, Muslim Council of Britain.

140. Ibid, 171.

141. www.mcb.org.uk/indexcensus.htm

142. *The Muslim News*, 28 February 2003.

143. Humayun Ansari, (2002), *Muslims in Britain*, p. 9, Minority Rights Group International, London.

144. The Runnymede Trust, (1997), *Islamophobia: Its Features and Dangers: A Consultation Paper*, p. 16, London.

145. Weller, P. Fieldman, A. and Purdam, K. *Religious Discrimination in England and Wales*, p. 77, Home Office Research Study 220, London, Home Office, 2001.

146. www.mcb.org.uk

147. Ibid.

148. Muhammad Anwar and Qadir Bakhsh, (2003), *British Muslims and State Policies*, p. 28, The Centre for Research and Ethnic Relations, University of Warwick.

149. Ibid, p. 38.

150. Bhikhu Parekh, *Muslims in Britain*, Prospect Magazine, July 2003.

151. Monitoring Minority Protection in the EU: *The Situation of Muslims in the UK*, (2002), p. 77, Open Society Institute.

152. The Parekh Report, (2000), *The Future of Multi-Ethnic Britain: Report of the Commission on the Future of Multi-Ethnic Britain*, p. 247, Profile Books Ltd.

153. Jenkins, R. (1967), *Racial Equality in Britain*, in Anthony Lester (Ed.), Essays and Speeches by Roy Jenkins, p. 267, Collins: London.

154. Tariq Ramadan, (1999), *To be a European Muslim*, p. 77, The Islamic Foundation, Leicester.

155. Qur'an 57:25.

156. Tariq Modood, (1997), *"Difference", Cultural Racism and Anti-Racism'*, in P. Werbner, and T. Modood (Eds), Debating Cultural Hybridity.

157. Qur'an 3:103.

158. Qur'an 49:13.

159. Christine E. Dobbin, (Ed.), (1970), *Basic Documents in the Development of Modern India and Pakistan*, 1835-1947, p. 8, London: Van Nostrand.

160. C.E. Von Grunebaum, (1962), *Modern Islam: The Search for Cultural Identity*, pp. 249-88, Berkeley: University of California Press.

161. Muhammad Abdul Bari, (2002), *The Greatest Gift: A Guide to*

Parenting from an Islamic Perspective, p. 43, Ta-Ha Publishers Ltd.

162. *Bayhaqi.*
163. Qur'an 3:64.
164. Qur'an 2:143.
165. The Parekh Report, (2000), *The Future of Multi-Ethnic Britain: Report of the Commission on the Future of Multi-Ethnic Britain*, p. 36, Profile Books Ltd.
166. Ibid. p. 38.
167. Qur'an 12:33.
168. Qur'an: 2:256.
169. Qur'an 20:114.
170. *Ibn Majah.*
171. *Tirmidhi.*
172. *Imam Ghazzali, Ihya Ulum-id- din, Book II*, p. 18, *New Delhi.*
173. Tariq Ramadan, (1999), *To be a European Muslim*, p. 121, *The Islamic Foundation, Leicester.*
174. Qur'an: 5:77.
175. Qur'an 5:8.
176. Qur'an 2:177, 3:36, 16:90, 17:26, 30:38, 42:23, 59:8.
177. Qur'an 2:83.
178. *Bukhari.*
179. Qur'an 4:1, 49:13.

BIBLIOGRAPHY

Abul Hasan Ali Nadwi, (1983), *Islam and the World*, IIFSO, Kuwait.

Adlin Adnan, (1999), *New Muslims in Britain*, Ta-Ha Publishers, London.

Albert Hourani, (1991), *Islam in European Thought*, Cambridge University Press.

Al-Bukhari, *Sahih al-Bukhari*, Translated by Dr. Muhammad Muhsin Khan (1997), Darusslam, Riyadh.

An-Nawawi, Imam (1998), *Riad-us-Salehin*, Islamic Book Service, Delhi.

Anthony Lester (Ed.), (1999), *Essays and Speeches by Roy Jenkins*, London: Collins.

Barbara Daly Metcalfe, (Ed.), (1996), *Making Muslim Space in North America and Europe,* University of California.

Christine E. Dobbin (Ed.), (1970), *Basic Documents in the Development of Modern India and Pakistan* 1835-1947, London: Van Nostrand.

C.E. Von Grunebaum, (1962), *Modern Islam: The Search for Cultural Identity*, Berkeley: University of California Press.

David Mason, (2000), *Race and Ethnicity in Modern Britain*, Oxford University Press.

Dilip Hiro, (1992), *Black British, White British: A History of Race relations in Britain*, Paladin, London.

Dr. S. M. Darsh (1980), *Muslims in Europe*, Ta-Ha Publishers, London.

Encyclopaedia Britannica, Copyright 1994-1999.

Eric Williams, (1964). *Capitalism and Slavery*, Andre Deutsch, London.

Ethnic Minorities in Britain: Diversity and Disadvantage, The Fourth National survey of Ethnic Minorities by Policy Studies Institute, (1997), London.

Franco Cardini, (2001), *Europe and Islam*, Blackwell.

Gainer, B., (1972), *The Alien Invasion: the origins of the Aliens Act of 1905*, Heinemann, London.

Foot, P., (1965), *Immigration and Race in British Politics*, Penguin Books

Gerald Parsons (Ed.), (1994), *The Growth of Religious Diversity – Britain from 1945*, Routledge, London.

Hall, S., et al, (Eds), (1992), *Modernity and its Future*, Polity, Cambridge.

Hans Kung, (2002), *Tracing the Way: Spiritual Dimensions of the World Religions*, translated by John Bowden, Continuum.

Home Office, (1975). *Racial Discrimination, Cmnd* 6234, HMSO, London.

Humayun Ansari, (2002), *Muslims in Britain*, Minority Rights Group International, London.

Ian S Markham and Tinu Ruparell (Eds,) (2001), *Encountering Religion*, Blackwell Publishers.

Imam Ghazali, *Ihya Ulum-id- din Book II*, New Delhi.

Imam Muslim, *Sahih Muslim*, Translated by Andul Hamid Siddiqi, (1990), Ashraf Islamic Publishers, Lahore.

Jackson, J. A., (1963), *The Irish in Britain*, Routledge.

John Esposito, (1988), *Islam: The Straight Path*, Oxford University Press.

Keith Ward, (1999), *Religion and Community*, Oxford University Press.

Laura Panketh, (2000), *Tackling Institutional Racism: Anti-racist Policies and Social Work Education and Training*, The Policy Press.

Macdonald, I., (1983), *Immigration Law and Practice in the United Kingdom*, Butterworths.

Malise Ruthven, (2000), *Islam in the World*, Penguin Books.

Monitoring Minority Protection in the EU: The Situation of Muslims in the UK, (2002), Open Society Institute.

Muhammad Anwar (1994), *Young Muslims in Britain: Attitudes, Educational*

Needs and Policy Implications, The Islamic Foundation, Leicester.

Muhammad Anwar and Qadir Bakhsh (2003), *British Muslims and State Policies, The centre for Research in Ethnic Relations*, University of Warwick.

Panikos Panayi, (1994), *Immigration, ethnicity and racism in Britain* 1815-1945, Manchester University Press.

Philip Lewis, (2000), *Islamic Britain: Religion, Politics and Identity among British Muslims*, I.B.Tauris.

Pickthall, Muhammad Marmaduke, *The Meaning of the Glorious Qur'an: Text and Explanatory Translation*, New American Library.

Professor Jeremy Black (Ed), (1999), *Encyclopedia of World History*, Parragon.

Richard Hatcher, (1995), *Racism in children's culture*, in 'Antiracism, Culture and Social Justice in Education', (Eds, Griffiths M and Tonya, B., Trentham Books.

Rose, E.J.B. et al. (1969), *Colour and Citizenship: A Report on British Race Relations*, Oxford University Press.

Sheridan Gilley W. J. Sheils (Eds), (1994), *A History of Religion in Britain*, Blackwell.

Solomos, J. (Ed.), (1990), *Race and Local politics*, Macmillan, Basingstoke.

Solomos, J., (1993), *Race and Racism in Britain*, Macmillan Press Ltd, London.

S. Allen and M. Macey (Eds), *Race and Social Policy*, Economic and Social Research Council, London.

Swann, Lord Michael (1985), *Education for All: Report of the Committee of Inquiry into the Education of Children from Ethnic Minority Groups, Cmnd* 9453, HMSO, London.

The Quest for Sanity: Reflections on September 11 *and the Aftermath*, (2002), Muslim Council of Britain.

The Stephen Lawrence Inquiry, Report of an Inquiry by Sir William Macpherson of Cluny, 1999.

Steve Bruce, (1995), *Religion in Modern Britain*, Oxford University Press.

Steven Vertovec and Alisdair Roger, (Eds.), (1998), *Muslim European Youth: Reproducing Ethnicity, Religion, Culture*, Ashgate Publishing Ltd.

Syed Ameer Ali, (1926), *A Short History of the Saracens*, Kitab Bhavan, New

INDEX